Positively Powerless

How a Forgotten Movement Undermined Christianity

L.L. Martin

L. L. Martin
Col. 3:1-2

WESTBOW
PRESS®
A DIVISION OF THOMAS NELSON
& ZONDERVAN

Scripture taken from the Holy Bible, NEW INTERNATIONAL VERSION®.
Copyright © 1973, 1978, 1984, 2011 by Biblica, Inc. All rights reserved worldwide.
Used by permission. NEW INTERNATIONAL VERSION® and NIV® are
registered trademarks of Biblica, Inc. Use of either trademark for the offering
of goods or services requires the prior written consent of Biblica US, Inc.

All Scripture quotations in this publications are from The Message.
Copyright © by Eugene H. Peterson 1993, 1994, 1995, 1996, 2000,
2001, 2002. Used by permission of NavPress Publishing Group.

WestBow Press books may be ordered through booksellers or by contacting:

WestBow Press
A Division of Thomas Nelson & Zondervan
1663 Liberty Drive
Bloomington, IN 47403
www.westbowpress.com
1 (866) 928-1240

Because of the dynamic nature of the Internet, any web addresses or
links contained in this book may have changed since publication and
may no longer be valid. The views expressed in this work are solely those
of the author and do not necessarily reflect the views of the publisher,
and the publisher hereby disclaims any responsibility for them.

Any people depicted in stock imagery provided by Thinkstock are models,
and such images are being used for illustrative purposes only.
Certain stock imagery © Thinkstock.

ISBN: 978-1-5127-2295-6 (sc)
ISBN: 978-1-5127-2297-0 (hc)
ISBN: 978-1-5127-2296-3 (e)

Library of Congress Control Number: 2015920512

Print information available on the last page.

WestBow Press rev. date: 12/29/2015

Contents

To

"him who loves us and
has freed us from our sins by his blood"

Revelation 1:5

Acknowledgments

If you had told me years ago that I would one day write a book, I'm not sure I would have believed it. Thanks to my immediate family: mom, dad, and brother. Books were all around our home. Reading and learning were encouraged. I'm appreciative of the advantages I had in this regard, as well as being raised in a Christian home with parents who carefully studied the Scripture.

Despite these advantages, writing a book is a daunting project. I am thankful for a number of individuals who valued my informal writing and encouraged me to write a book.

Special thanks to Bob Martin, Carole Chaput, Tim Fall, Trevor Bernardo, and Saralyn Temple who read my manuscript and offered input on improving it. Bob Martin is my husband and has always supported me in my life endeavors even when the undertakings were unconventional. Saralyn's assistance with grammar and syntax was invaluable. I am grateful to Sherri Jason who helped brainstorm titles for the book, and to her I am indebted for the title. Saralyn and Sherri are friends from my distant past, and we reconnected recently through social media. I am deeply appreciative that they were willing to assist me despite our being out of touch for so long. I met Carole in seminary classes, and her spiritual and theological insights have been vital. Thanks to Jackie Willey, Laura Droege, and Suzanne Burden who offered advice and encouragement in regards to publishing. And to anyone I have inadvertently overlooked, thank you.

Introduction

In the process of writing, I was asked about the topic of my book and found it hard to answer such a seemingly easy question. Saying it was a critique of the positive thinking movement from a Christian perspective would typically elicit puzzlement. Aren't Christians supposed to be hopeful and encouraging? However, this is not the simple idea of having a good or bad attitude in life.

I bet you have muttered "think positive" before an uncertain moment or stated this maxim in encouragement to a friend. Have you ever paused to think about what you are *really* saying and the implications of it? How exactly will positive thoughts help? You might think I am over-analyzing the issue. Yet there is a long and extensive history behind the idea of positive thinking, and it reveals how the expression "think positive" became a part of the American vernacular. Positive thinking was a vast movement which took the twentieth century by storm and radically changed American culture. Evidence of this philosophy is everywhere once you are aware of it. It can hide in plain view because it became such a natural way of thinking in our society.

Secular and sacred motivational approaches gained prominence in mid-twentieth century America, but these things developed from an older movement named "New Thought" whose beginnings are mostly forgotten—somehow passing out of common historical memory. New Thought believed in a mystical power of thoughts that could alter our outward reality. Of particular concern to the Christian are the movement's roots in occult, mystical, and Eastern religious ideas that are in distinct conflict with Christianity. My research into this was eye-opening, and the first chapter will delve into this disconcerting background.

This non-biblical philosophy invaded the church during the twentieth century and continues to be influential long after the fact. Much of this "invasion" was subtle, coming in by the side door as Christians themselves were influenced by it. These teachings were often cushioned in biblical language—which made them harder to detect—yet there is little excuse for how so many believers fell for it. The core temptation is an ancient one, and we should have been on better guard against it—to be elaborated upon in chapter two.

The book contains content we might prefer to avoid such as chapters on pride and sin. Positive thinking has *itself* contributed to our discomfort about these core Christian beliefs and blurred our spiritual vision. Evading our sin makes it difficult to see our need of a Savior. When the church catches the spirit of the age, it becomes spiritually weak.

While intended to be a positive movement, it can lead to disillusionment and despair. Have you ever felt like a failure in the Christian life or that you must hide your struggles with sin? Maybe you have been on a perpetual search for a spiritual secret that would finally bring you that evasive victory. Perhaps you sensed something was not quite right in certain approaches to faith but were unable to put your finger on it. The positive thinking mindset is at work in these scenarios.

Its cultural impact led to Christians developing false expectations or illusions about themselves and their spirituality. A quest for what we might become in life took precedence. It turned us inward and distracted us from the hope found in Jesus Christ. The central message of Christianity is not about becoming a better you, but about Jesus who lived a perfect life for you.

The aim of this book is to be an advocate for *neither* positivity nor negativity, but for biblical balance and realism. Positive thinking tilted Christianity off balance, and we need the scales to be realigned. The chapter entitled "The Already but Not Yet" will further explain this crucial idea that has been neglected by many. We are lopsided Christians. Present and future aspects of our faith have been confused, and this has distorted our perceptions of life in this world. We are supposed to feel a bit restless and disappointed in this life. Maybe that sounds unhopeful or gloomy to you, but it is neglect of biblical balance that actually dashes our hope by creating false ones. The best life is not now but in the future on the new heaven and earth. Hebrews 11:1 reminds us that "faith is confidence in what we hope for and assurance about what we do not see" (New International Version).

We've been led to believe that any form of negativity is wrong, but thinking about true and good things may not necessarily be positive. Sometimes the truth hurts. It convicts. It may humble us and open our eyes. We need these humbling moments more often than we care to admit and in order to grow into the likeness of our Savior.

Christianity is all about paradox: power is found through weakness, to live we must die to self, and to be lifted high we must stoop low. The Christian life is uniquely different from our natural inclinations and in stark conflict with the positive thinking paradigm. Some aspects of this book may seem a bit hard-hitting but it is only because we have become so accustomed to the pervasive cultural dogma of self-affirmation and self-fulfillment. Several chapters will address the paradoxes and tensions of the Christian life in an attempt to bring clarity about the nature of Christian humility and how we should view ourselves as Christians.

This book seeks to offer hope. A movement that claimed to offer power turned out to be powerless, and the only solution is in the power of the gospel of Jesus Christ. As Christians, we must continue to live in light of the gospel by which we were saved. Chapter 8 will delve into the great doctrine of justification by faith which is tremendously relevant to how we live our lives. When we live in light of the gospel, it creates a radical new dynamic for confident Christian living.

It was awkward to write about certain topics such as pride and self-righteousness. You feel hypocritical writing about a problem when you have not conquered it yourself. Yet who is really qualified to write about these things except our Lord Jesus Christ who lived a perfect life on our behalf? Please know I am a fellow sinner on this road with you.

Thank you for obtaining a copy of *Positively Powerless*. I hope it will give you a new or heightened awareness of how positive thinking has been harmful to the Christian faith. Throughout the book, I have been evasive about *current* Christian ministries and individuals. Instead of telling you what to think about the teachings of a specific author or pastor, I hope it will help you exercise personal discernment with *any* Christian material to which you expose yourself. Are you being encouraged to fix your thoughts on Jesus, or is it just giving you more of yourself? As the author of Hebrews implores: "Therefore, holy brothers and sisters, who share in the heavenly calling, fix your thoughts on Jesus." (Hebrews 3:1).

L.L. Martin

Chapter 1

Thou Shalt Not Be Negative

God is not under any obligation to make me succeed.
—Timothy Keller

It is appropriate that a prosperity gospel be born in the hedonistic,
self-centered, get rich-quick milieu of modern American society.
We are, by nature, pagan. Either our religion will transform
us or we will transform our religion to suit our sympathies.
—Michael Horton

Think positive! An optimistic outlook seems as American as apple
pie. Type "positive thinking" into your web browser or start perusing
books for sale, and you'll soon be lost in a sea of self-help articles and
books related to the power of positive thinking. Of course, we don't
always take the positive thinking mantra seriously—who hasn't
rolled their eyes at some late-night infomercial selling a motivational
program? Yet this general approach to life and the idea that our
thoughts are influential is ingrained into our culture and is a part of
our modern psyche. But did you know this was not always the case?

Maybe you've heard the name Norman Vincent Peale. It was this
Protestant minister who turned "positive thinking" into a household

idea back in mid-twentieth century America.[1] However, Peale was simply riding the wave of a mind-power movement that in actuality began about one hundred years previously in the mid-nineteenth century. Prior to this time there was no common notion that a positive view of yourself and your future was a critical key to success. Concepts such as hard work, thrift, and character were valued as the way to get ahead in life. It isn't that these concepts are no longer considered beneficial today, but the importance of positive thinking would have been a strange and unfamiliar idea in early America.

As someone who enjoys history, I've never understood why it is such a dreaded subject for many people. When asked about my favorite subject as a child, my response of "history" usually induced surprise. Nonetheless, we need to consider the historical background and development of positive thinking in America. Several authors provide us with a fascinating and startling peek into the beginnings of this movement.[2] I was truly mesmerized by all that I learned, and I'll do my best to share some of the highlights. As an added bonus, you'll discover the history of the word *mesmerized*! As Christians, it is imperative that we understand the underlying philosophies from which positive thinking developed.

Mitch Horowitz has written an extensive history of the positive thinking movement. He summarizes positive thinking by emphasizing that it did not merely influence American culture, but did much more:

> Positive thinking entered the ground water of American life. It became the unifying element of all aspects of the American search for meaning. The shapers of positive thinking fundamentally altered how we see ourselves today—psychologically, religiously, commercially, and politically. Their story is the backstory of modern America. Peer into any corner of current American life, and you'll find

the positive thinking outlook….It forms the
foundation of business motivation, self-help, and
therapeutic spirituality, including within the world
of evangelism.[3]

Perhaps you are thinking this is a passé topic. In a certain way,
you are correct. The positive thinking movement no longer exists. It
is dead—an artifact of the twentieth century—but this is precisely
why we need to carefully consider it.

Somewhere along the line it was no longer necessary for anyone
to consider the value of the positive thinking mantra and to make
a choice to accept it. It had been
absorbed by osmosis into our society.
It was no longer a movement but had
instead become a part of who we are
and how we think as Americans.
When something attaches itself

> Positive thinking may be
> dead, but it lives on and
> yields its power in subtle
> but significant ways.

to the very fabric of a culture, its sway can be forgotten or go
undetected because it is a natural way of thinking. Positive thinking
may be dead, but it lives on and yields its power in subtle but
significant ways. The passage of time can also provide beneficial
perspective and clarity as we look back and consider the influence
of the past. Let's step back in time…

Positive thinking ideas initially grew out of distinctly occult
and mystical subcultures in mid-nineteenth century America. Yet
the impetus behind these things goes back further, to eighteenth
century Europe. For example, the teachings of a European scientist,
mystic, and Protestant theologian named Emanuel Swedenborg
became influential. He claimed to have received a new revelation
from Jesus Christ through a series of visions, rejected the Trinity,
and thought there was a "divine influx" that permeated nature and
humanity. He also claimed to be a clairvoyant with a special ability
to look into the spirit world.

Another European was a physician named Franz Anton Mesmer (take note of that last name Mesmer!) who theorized that all of life contained an invisible fluid—an unseen energy—that he called "animal magnetism." When this fluid was out of balance, illness resulted, and he would place people in a trance-like state to realign the unseen energy and resolve the illness. Coincidentally, Mesmer also discovered that when these people were in a trance, they were receptive to his suggestions or commands. (Yes, this eventually became hypnotism.) Mesmer's ideas were expanded by others who followed in his footsteps. One protégé of Mesmer gave students graduating from his class in mesmerism an affirmation that stated, in part, "I believe in the existence within myself of a power. From this belief derives my will to exert it. The entire doctrine of animal magnetism is contained in two words: believe and want."[4] These eighteenth-century European ideas "crossed the pond" and became influential in certain areas of mid-nineteenth century America, taking on a life of their own.

From Europe to America

Phineas Quimby was a clockmaker in New England who believed he had overcome a personal health problem through his own mind-over-matter methods. He came in contact with a mesmerist, and this stimulated his interest in it. Quimby developed his own theories of "mental healing"—the use of the mind in healing physical ailments—and he began traveling and healing the sick. His ideas became particularly prominent throughout New England. While Quimby could be an unfamiliar name to you, you may have heard of Mary Baker Eddy. She was a patient and student of Quimby, and Eddy founded the Christian Science church. Christian Science "reading rooms," located in many major cities, are about all that remains of this once-thriving movement. A joke made about Christian Science is that it was neither Christian nor scientific. Disease was perceived more like a mental error or an illusion rather than a physical disorder. Unlike Quimby, Eddy attempted to blend Christianity and mental healing ideas, yet Christian Science rejected core Christian doctrines such as the Trinity, the deity of Christ, and the necessity of Christ's death to atone for sin.

Warren Felt Evans was another key individual in these early years. He was a Protestant minister who became swayed by the teachings of Swedenborg. Followers of Swedenborg's teachings were typically attracted to Quimby's ideas as well. Evans described faith as a force, and he taught that the power of your faith could cause prayers to come true in reality. His beliefs as they evolved over time became increasingly distanced from orthodox Christian doctrine. He perceived Jesus as a human who had a vivid consciousness of "god" within, and he believed that we too could access this divine energy within us.[5] Evans wrote a series of books that helped create interest in mental healing ideas, such as one entitled *Esoteric Christianity and Mental Therapeutics*.

I came across a book of essays from this time period (1889) written by Prentice Mulford, which was re-printed in 2007 under the category of New Age books. One chapter is entitled "The God in Yourself," and Mulford had similar ideas to Evans's. He viewed Jesus Christ as a human who had accessed the divine power of the universe within himself. Christ learned to concentrate his thoughts to the point where his thoughts could change reality—such as the miracles he performed. Christ was perceived as an example for us of the possibility of using our own thoughts in this powerful way. Mulford also believed in a type of reincarnation. In each life your mind grows more powerful, and humankind is mentally ascending upward.[6]

As time progressed during the late nineteenth and early twentieth century, these various ideas developed into an actual movement known as New Thought. New Thought philosophies were often an eclectic combination of ideas pulled from Christianity, Eastern religions, transcendentalism, Kabbalah, spiritism, mysticism, and other esoteric traditions. Its diverse nature makes it hard to precisely pin down. New Thought was not an official group but rather a loose affiliation of authors, speakers, and practitioners who branched out with their own unique mind-power ideas. New Thought moved beyond the initial emphasis of using the mind to heal physical illness, and it saw the power of the mind as able to alleviate a variety of problems in everyday life.

> Send out your thought—thought is a force, and it has occult power of unknown proportions.
> —Ralph Waldo Trine

To be clear, this was not about using our intelligence to solve problems—it was about actually viewing the mind as a force unto itself. The mind was perceived as *the* controlling factor in human life. The concept was that thoughts were "things" that possessed a mystical type of causative power to influence reality. Your thoughts could actually alter the circumstances surrounding your life by "attracting" events or occurrences. Ralph Waldo Trine was a prolific New Thought writer, who described it this way:

> Send out your thought—thought is a force, and it has occult power of unknown proportions when rightly used and wisely directed—send out your thought that the right situation or the right work will come to you at the right time, in the right way.[7]

In New Thought, "god" was typically viewed as an impersonal force or principle as opposed to a personal being. Ultimately it was about the improvement of humanity and having a more satisfying and successful life through thought-directed techniques.

I've noticed a recent trend of people directing their thoughts *to someone* who is experiencing a difficult time or needing a good outcome: "sending positive thoughts your way." What exactly is meant by this? Possibly they only want the person to know they are being thought about and not forgotten. If that is what is meant, it should be worded that way: "thinking of you." The wording of sending out positive thoughts connotes something altogether different; it reflects New Thought, elevating the power of thoughts to mystical heights whether or not that is realized by the speaker. As Christians, we should consider the implications of our words and not use this phraseology.

This trend is related to a popular book and movie entitled *The Secret* from 2006 which is modernized New Thought ideology. The book was featured on *The Oprah Winfrey Show*, stayed on the *New York Times* bestseller list for three years, and has sold twenty million copies. Its cultural impact has been substantial. The author of *The Secret*, Rhonda Byrne, was influenced by a New Thought book from the early twentieth century. Byrne promotes the typical New Thought idea that we can harness a special power in the universe through the use of our thoughts and "attract" the outcomes we desire in every area of our life.

Norman Vincent Peale

As the twentieth century progressed, New Thought slowly moved away from the unconventional aspects that distanced it from mainstream people and became something like an optimistic motivational philosophy. As these changes gradually occurred, it made its way into mainstream American culture with its influence spilling into traditional religion, business meetings, political campaigns, and living rooms. It was Norman Vincent Peale in the 1950's who was most influential in bringing "positive thinking" to the masses. As a Protestant minister, he blended positive thinking concepts with biblical references and language. This, along with his down-to-earth approach, made his message appealing to traditional church going folks and the general public.

Peale's core message was that, besides being forgiven, you can achieve and succeed in life too. While he carefully cushioned his positive thinking teachings in scriptural terms, his beliefs were centered in New Thought ideas. The discerning and observant reader could pick up on this in his best-selling book *The Power of Positive Thinking*. While some of the New Thought content is subtle, other is more direct. For example, Peale states "When you expect the best, you release a magnetic force in your mind which by a law of attraction tends to bring the best to you."[8] Similarly, Peale speaks of prayer as sending out vibrations from one person *to another* and to God. He says the air or universe is filled with vibrations, and we need positive vibes through prayer to utilize this spiritual force.[9] Please don't miss that in addition to prayer involving God; it involves vibrations between two people. This is not biblical prayer, and prayer should be directed to God alone.

By the mid-twentieth century, positive thinking became "the American creed" as Horowitz titles one of his chapters.[10] As a result, new fields developed such as pastoral counseling, business motivation, and all varieties of the self-help genre. These things which are so commonplace today did not always exist, or at least not in the ubiquitous way that they do now. Not everyone is a fan of positive thinking, and there have been critics of it all along. Regardless, we are all products of our culture and of the past, and our thoughts are held hostage to these pervasive ideas.

Positive Thinking and Christianity

Can you see why studying history is important? If you have been *unknowingly* influenced by something from the past, an awareness of history is the only way you'll discover it. In addition, if we are not distinctly aware and observant of culture, we can end up conforming to it without knowing it. As Christians, we should wonder: How has the positive thinking mentality affected us individually and corporately? How has it altered our perceptions and expectations of the Christian life? Churches of all types, from mainline to evangelical, have come under the sway of some aspect of the power of positive thinking.

There is a difference between the earlier New Thought beliefs which were grounded in the occult or Eastern religious ideas, and the more benign motivational methods that developed later. However, the fact remains that the benign approaches developed out of a syncretistic, non-biblical belief system. This should give us pause and create genuine concern. Multiple aspects of New Thought and the background behind it are in significant conflict with biblical Christianity:

- the authority given to extra biblical revelation
- the idea that God is a force rather than a personal being
- denial of the full deity of Jesus Christ
- denial of the Trinity
- denial of the providence or sovereignty of God

Consider that when the mind is seen as *the* controlling factor in life, it displaces God in one way or another. We become like gods with an ability to control events through our thoughts. One early New Thought writer stated: "All power is from within and therefore under our control."[11] While later positive thinking approaches were less objectionable, the fact remains that they elevate our thoughts and give them more authority than is wise for a Christian and encourage a distinctly self-centered outlook towards life. Hebrews 3:1 says we should fix our thoughts on Jesus. An adherence to positive thinking notions leads to our thoughts being fixed on ourselves, our success, our happiness, and our personal desires.

We need to fully grasp how influential the New Thought movement became in Christianity as it put down roots that spread insidiously beneath the spiritual terrain over time. It could be considered one of the most harmful things to have affected Christianity in the twentieth century. Yet, for the most part, it is an unknown or forgotten movement.

Evangelical scholars Jones and Woodbridge have carefully traced the rise of the prosperity gospel in the mid-twentieth century from New Thought ideas. I recommend their book to you entitled: *Health, Wealth, & Happiness, Has the Prosperity Gospel Overshadowed the Gospel of Christ?* The connection between New Thought and the prosperity gospel may not be initially apparent because the concepts were re-packaged with familiar and reassuring Christian language. Prosperity gospel teachers may not have knowingly done this either, but they were influenced by the culture and failed to realize it. Isolated Bible verses were taken out of context to support an optimistic view of humanity and success in this life. This led to a blending of Christian and New Thought principles even though the two clearly conflict.

While the prosperity gospel is limited to a certain segment of Christianity, some of the ideas weaved their way into mainstream evangelicalism. This book is not a critique of the prosperity gospel but of the "positivity gospel" that developed in relation to it. While the focus is not so directly on prosperity, Christianity can be presented in a "therapeutic" sense with God being like a personal cheerleader whose primary concern is our success in life. Remember the aforementioned emphasis of Peale: besides being forgiven, you can succeed too. It would appear that we have transformed our religion to suit our sympathies. Consider this sampling of recent (2004-2014) book titles from Christian authors:

Better Than Good: Creating a Life You Can't Wait to Live
It's Your Time: Activate Your Faith, Achieve Your Dreams, and Increase in God's Favor

Power Thoughts: 12 Strategies to Win the Battle of the Mind
A Better Way to Think: Using Positive Thoughts to Change Your Life
You Can, You Will: 8 Undeniable Qualities of a Winner
Jesus, Life Coach: Learn from the Best

While I chose overt titles to make a point, a plethora of Christian books fall under the "self-help" or "Christian living" category. There is a pronounced individualistic, egocentric standpoint with far too many Christian books and no shortage of ideas for leading a satisfying Christian life. It is like a success syndrome infected the church at large. To be discussed in chapter 7, the self-esteem movement that developed in the 1970's can also be linked back to New Thought ideas, and it spilled into the church as well.

> The quest for what we might become in life pushed Jesus to the sideline.

Christian author Philip Yancey, known for his honest and down-to-earth attitude is not afraid to tackle tough topics that some Christians evade. In his book *Disappointment with God*, he points out that there is a large gap between what people *expect* from their Christian faith and what they *actually* experience. Yancey states, "From a steady diet of books, sermons, and personal testimonies, all promising triumph and success, they learn to expect dramatic evidence of God working in their lives."[12] Consider the implications of a sermon on Noah entitled "How courage can help *you* conquer a storm" or one on Rebekah entitled "How generosity can multiply *your* impact." Of course, there are personal lessons we can apply to our individual lives, but the spotlight is moved from God to us and makes Scripture about our success in life. Is that what Christianity is really all about? No! Christianity is about Jesus Christ and all that was accomplished for us in his life, death, and resurrection. It is emphasized in Colossians 1:18 that Jesus must be supreme. He must have the first place in everything. The quest for what we might become in life pushed Jesus to the sideline.

Related to the focus on success, there can be a false perception that the Christian life can be easy—hardship can be evaded—if we only do certain things or have a strong enough faith. Rather than believing there is power in our thoughts (as in New Thought) some encourage clinging to the power of our faith. Problems are blamed on a weak faith. While our faith and prayers are influential in this life, Bible verses about trouble and tribulation are conveniently overlooked (John 16:33; Acts 14:22).[13] Christians in other time periods of history often had a *polar opposite perspective* living with an expectation of difficulty in this world but looking to their future hope in Christ. Faith is trust in God irrespective of our circumstances, remembering that the "best life" is yet to come on the new heaven and earth. As Christian author Randy Alcorn directly states: "Christians should expect to suffer more, not less, since they suffer under the Fall and as followers of Christ. If your goal is to avoid suffering in this life, then following Christ will not help you."[14] Ouch! But a needed reminder and rebuke.

As the line of a beloved old hymn states, sometimes the wrong seems oft so strong in this world.[15] We can wonder about God's involvement in it all. Theodicy, or why a good God allows suffering and evil, must be addressed by every belief system. Randy Alcorn makes another astute observation when he points out that too many evangelical churches have failed to teach people to think biblically about the realities of evil and suffering. This failure has left Christians unprepared for the harsh realities of life and made them vulnerable to abandoning the faith when hardship comes.[16]

While theodicy is a detailed issue, it is fascinating that Horowitz points out that Norman Vincent Peale's "philosophy of positivity and self-worth was incapable of meeting life in all of its difficulties and tragedies. His outlook did not include a theology of suffering."[17] As already noted, Peale's methods were a blend of Christian and New Thought ideas. New Thought philosophies were a failure at explaining tragedies in life, often viewing them as an illusion, and their explanations were contradictory. If your positive thoughts should have prevented tragedy, how can you explain very real calamity in spite of it? This can be a downright cruel philosophy as it makes adversity the fault of the victim.

Mixing Christianity with other belief systems is always problematic. Jesus Christ was inclusive with people but exclusive when it came to truth (John 14:6). A syncretistic Christianity creates confusion and leads people away from the truth. The positive thinking mentality is no doubt a reason that some Christians have been unprepared for the harsh realities of life. This is sad. Biblical Christianity is the worldview best able to meet the tragedies of life and provide a robust theology of suffering. Delving into theodicy is beyond the scope of this book, but I highly recommend Randy Alcorn's book *If God is Good: Faith in the Midst of Suffering and Evil*.

We cannot simplistically blame these concerns exclusively on New Thought and the power of positive thinking. Causes are multifaceted, and other explanations are part of the picture. Yet the influence is there, and it has been overlooked or underestimated by cultural blindness. I am also *not* insinuating that Christian motivational books or sermons are occultist. Neither am I suggesting that they have no value whatsoever. While much of this material can lead us astray in the Christian life, some may possess a more accurate biblical foundation and conceivably encourage us— in limited doses. Nevertheless, many of us need to take a step back and consider whether we actually hold a distinctly Christian worldview in how we are perceiving life in general and the spiritual life in particular.

The Real Origin of Positive Thinking

As believers, it seems our radar should have been more sensitive to the problems of the positive thinking movement. This proclivity has existed from the beginning or even before the beginning. Consider the Fall of humanity in Genesis chapter three. In verses 4 and 5, the serpent says "You will not certainly die…For God knows that when you eat from it your eyes will be opened, and you will be like God, knowing good and evil."

Essentially, Satan tempted them with the power of positive thinking! Didn't he? Even though God spent time in the garden with Adam and Eve (Genesis 3:8), it was not enough for them. Imagine living in such an ideal place and having such intimate commune with your Creator. Adam and Eve were created in the image of God, yet they wanted to become even more like God. They wanted to know more and reach toward their full potential. As we all know, their yielding to this temptation did not turn out well for humanity.

We can go even farther back in time before the creation of humanity and consider the angels. Angels are also created beings. Most evangelical scholars believe that Satan was once an angel that rebelled and fell from his angelic position.[18] Satan became occupied with his own splendor and fell because of pride. He desired to be like God or to take God's place. Isn't it interesting that Satan tempted Adam and Eve in a similar way? This is an inherent weakness of creatures.

The temptation is echoed in the New Thought movement: humanity can ascend and realize their loftiest goals. The chronic human problem is not that we think too lowly of ourselves, but that we think too highly of ourselves. I remember a t-shirt I saw years ago that said, "There are two things sure in life: there is a God, and you are not him!" It was meant to be funny but made an accurate point. We seem prone to forget our status as creatures. Extreme caution should be exercised with any teaching that confuses the status of man and God.

Questions for Reflection and Discussion

1. "If we are not distinctly aware and observant of culture, we can end up conforming to it without knowing it." There is danger in both over-immersing and under-immersing ourselves in secular culture. On which side do you tend to err? How can we maintain a spiritually healthy balance?

2. New Thought beliefs were eclectic, a little of this and a little of that. What are the dangers of a belief system that has no central authority, text, or creeds?

3. Many people adhere to modern adaptations of New Thought, such as *The Secret*. What is the appeal? Why do you think people are drawn to it?

4. Have you been influenced by New Thought and positive thinking in ways you did not realize before you read this chapter, particularly in your Christian life?

Chapter 2

A Beast Most Savage

In reality, there is, perhaps, not one of our natural passions
so hard to subdue as pride. Disguise it, struggle with it, beat it
down, stifle it, mortify it as much as one pleases, it is still alive,
and will every now and then peep out and show itself...even
if I could conceive that I had completely overcome it, I should
probably be proud of my humility. —Benjamin Franklin

Our last contest is against the spirit of pride. Albeit it is the last
disease we have to fight and the closing member of the list, yet
in time and origin it is first of all. It is a beast most savage, and
fiercer than all the other: its worst temptations attack the perfect
and it devours with its most deadly bites those who have all but
reached the crown and sum of all virtues.
—St. John the Cassian

As we observed, Satan wanted to be like God, and he passed this
sin on to the human race. The positive thinking approach fed on
this human weakness, and the movement thrived as a result. The
universality of pride throughout time is undeniable, and we need
to carefully consider it. From Genesis 3 onward in the Bible, we

can observe the destructive nature of pride at work in the lives of individuals, families, and nations. Influential theologians and teachers throughout church history have viewed pride as the root of sin and as Satan's ultimate tool of temptation.

In his defense of faith in the early church entitled *The City of God,* Augustine characterized pride as the great political enemy that wanted to unseat God and enthrone itself. C.S. Lewis, in his apologetic book *Mere Christianity*, emphasizes that the essence of sin is pride. He states that "Pride leads to every other vice; it is the complete anti-God state of mind."[19] In pride we are self-absorbed; it breeds envy and discontent and creates a chain reaction of trouble. Lewis also points out that there is no fault we are more likely to overlook in ourselves. Other people are prideful—not us! Yet, being annoyed by another person's pride is actually indicative that we have a pride problem too. If we were truly humble, we would not care. If you have not read *Mere Christianity* in a long time, it is worthwhile to re-read the chapter on pride.

In Matthew 20, it says that the disciples James and John, along with their mother, came to Jesus and asked him for special seats of honor in the kingdom with Jesus. Jesus indicates in the passage that this was an inappropriate request for several reasons. However, it is the response of the other disciples that we want to take note of—it says that when the other ten heard about it, they were filled with indignation against James and John. The point made by C.S. Lewis is evident here. I think we typically read this passage and consider *only* James and John at fault. We relate to the anger of the ten! Yet the resentment of the other disciples was rooted in the same underlying pride exhibited by James and John. James and John should not have sought a position of honor where they would be served, and the others should not have been so upset at the idea of having to be their servants. Jesus reminds them in verses 26-28 that greatness in his kingdom is for those who serve.

A Christian should not be disturbed by the idea of serving or humbly taking a lower position before others. In an inconsistent way, leadership remains a focus in Christianity. There are an abundant number of publications and conferences about Christian leadership. Some of these things are helpful, and biblical leadership principles can be taught, but it seems a contradiction to use the word leadership. Maybe instead of the word leadership, these publications or events would better be labeled with the word servanthood. How about a servanthood conference? Jesus was a leader, but the Gospels emphasize that he came not to be served by others but to be a servant and to give his life (Mark 10:45). Jesus said in Luke 14:11, "For all those who exalt themselves will be humbled, and those who humble themselves will be exalted." Christianity turns everything upside down, and believers should not be absorbed with authority and position.

> How about a servanthood conference?

Ensnared by Self-Deception

I've also heard it said that the essence of sin is denial, which seems a different way of explaining the same concept. Have you ever thought about how easy it is to be self-deceived? Self-deception is insidious and hard to detect. If you come to the realization that you are self-deceived about something, then you are no longer self-deceived. It is easier to note sin *out there* than sin in ourselves. In pride, we think of every way possible to deny our sin. We rationalize it, make excuses for it, or conveniently forget it. I appreciate how Cornelius Plantinga, Jr. says it:

> Self-deception is a shadowy phenomenon by which
> we pull the wool over some part of our own

psyche….We become our own dupes…We know the truth—and yet we do not know it, because we persuade ourselves of its opposite.[20]

In the opening chapters of the book of Revelation, we can read seven brief letters that were written to churches that existed in what is now modern-day Turkey. Most of the churches were praised for what they were doing right, but were also critiqued for what they were doing wrong. The church of Laodicea in chapter 3 was sorely self-deceived. Their self-evaluation was drastically different from how Jesus evaluated them. They saw themselves as rich and in need of nothing, while Jesus saw them as wretched, miserable, poor, blind, and naked. Words were not minced! Sometimes we all need to be jolted out of our complacency or metaphorically wacked upside the head.

> We are enticed by pride, and ensnared by self-deception.

How have you become your own dupe? What you see as a personal strength, others may perceive as a weakness. Maybe you see yourself as clever, but others see you as sly. Maybe you see yourself as having a strong work ethic, but others see you as neglectful of your family. Maybe you see yourself as confident, but others perceive you as arrogant. Maybe you see yourself as discerning, but others observe a critical spirit. In pride, we have pulled the wool over our eyes in one way or another.

I see an integral connection between pride and self-deception, and each feed upon the other. We are enticed by pride, and ensnared by self-deception. Our pride prevents us from admitting our sin and causes us to perceive ourselves as better than other people. These false perceptions are self-deceptions fueled by pride. A dulled sense of sin is dangerous (to be elaborated upon in chapter 3) and hinders our ability to see our need of a Savior, to grasp the wonders of God's grace, and make progress in the Christian life.

A "topical Bible" is one which groups together Bible verses by topic, and it can prove to be a helpful study or devotional resource. It is convicting to read through ten pages of verses related to the issue of pride, self-presumption, and self-exaltation. We can't say the Scriptures have failed to caution us about it. The Bible from beginning to end is interwoven with content on the dangers of pride and the importance of humility. The opposite does not hold true, and we do not observe warnings about failing to have a high enough opinion of our self. This should remove any doubt about the weakness of humanity and where we need to exercise caution.

We can observe the downfalls of pride in varied biblical characters such as Pharaoh, King Uzziah, King Hezekiah, Ahithophel, Naaman, Haman, Nebuchadnezzar, and King Herod. The prophets denounced the pride of nations such as Moab, Babylon, Judah, and Israel.[21] In the Psalms and wisdom literature, there is repeated condemnation of arrogance and its dangers. It is expounded that pride:

- is detested by God (Proverbs 16:5).
- keeps God at a distance (Psalm 138:6).
- creates strife (Proverbs 13:10).
- brings disgrace or bondage (Psalm 73:6; Proverbs 11:2).
- leads to mistreatment of the weak (Psalm 10:2).
- leads to destruction (Proverbs 16:18).

While both Testaments warn against pride, I perceive a different emphasis in the Old and New Testaments. While the Old contains strong warnings about the dangers of pride, the New inversely focuses on the importance of humility and other similar traits such as self-denial, servanthood, and submission.

God Is Humble, We Are Proud

There are almost forty references to humility in the New Testament, whether the direct word or in concept. This should not surprise us in light of the core belief of Christianity: the Incarnation of God the Son. In the New Testament we observe the ultimate example of humility. As *The Message* amusingly words John 1:14, "The Word became flesh and blood, and moved into the neighborhood." The Creator became a creature. Have you ever really pondered that fact? It wasn't until later in my life that the profound mystery and miracle of the Incarnation really moved me. It is not debasing to humble yourself; it is Godlike to humble yourself! Mark McMinn takes note of the startling contrast:

> Our pride—our tendency to perceive ourselves as better than we are, our inflated self-assessments— demonstrates how much we want to be like God. Meanwhile, God—the eternal and majestic Creator, filled with all power, knowledge, and goodness— empties himself in the form of Jesus, even to the point of a violent and horrific death for trumped-up charges. In Augustine's words: 'God is already humble though man is still proud.' It is absurd. [22]

Yes, it is absurd. God moved into the neighborhood, and we want to ascend it. For years, I completely missed the main point of Philippians two. As someone more academically minded, I always thought of it as the theological chapter on the kenosis: how Jesus limited himself and became human. *But that is the secondary point.* Doctrine was not the primary point at all. Doctrine was being used as an illustration, and what we believe must affect how we live. We are to be humble because Jesus was humble. Philippians 2:3-5 states:

> Do nothing out of selfish ambition or vain conceit.
> Rather, in humility value others above yourselves,
> not looking to your own interests but each of you to
> the interests of the others. In your relationships with
> one another, have the same mindset as Christ Jesus.

Do we have the mindset of Jesus? We should do *nothing* from selfish ambition or vain conceit. Jesus called his followers to radical lives of self-denial (Mark 8:34), not self-centeredness or self-promotion. This is reinforced throughout the New Testament. We are exhorted to be clothed in humility, and to submit to one another out of reverence for Christ.[23] It should be noted that the adjective selfish is before the word ambition. Ambition can get a bad name, but there is nothing wrong with having ambitions in life. The concern is whether they are Godly ambitions or if they consume us in a selfish way, distracting us from what matters. Humility is more than having a modest view of ourselves. It is a way of life where we put others first and seek to serve them, just as our Savior did when he came into this world.

A Bible dictionary entry on pride states that "The emphasis placed on pride, and its converse humility, is a distinctive feature of biblical religion, unparalleled in other religions or ethical systems."[24] Since Christians worship the God that uniquely humbled himself by becoming human, this emphasis should not be a surprise. If God so humbled himself, certainly his followers should be humble too. The concept of "Seven Deadly Sins" can be traced back in church history, and pride is perceived as the most serious of the sins and the source of all the others. Key historical churchmen (Roman Catholic, Eastern Orthodox, and Protestant alike) taught that pride was a deadly vice.

Yet when is the last time you heard a sermon series or read a biblical book explicitly about pride and humility? Maybe pride or humility is briefly touched on, but is it expounded upon in any detail? Most likely not, or it happens infrequently. It is no longer a distinctive feature of biblical religion. The winds shifted in the twentieth century as the church increasingly came under the power of the positive thinking mentality. Of course, pride has been a problem throughout time, but in the past humility was generally admired. However, we live in a proud age where it can make us uncomfortable to speak of humility, and we worry about creating low self-esteem. A positive view of self is emphasized to the neglect of a more cautious view of ourselves. There is an odd obsession with self-esteem in our culture that will be elaborated upon in chapter seven.

> We have been so taken in by the spirit of our age that this distinctive feature of biblical religion troubles us.

I once observed outright aversion for teaching being done on Isaiah 6 which emphasized the humble state of humanity before the majestic God. We have been so taken in by the spirit of our age that this distinctive feature of biblical religion troubles us. I've interacted with *non-believers* who clearly perceive the clash between Christianity and the message of the positivity gospel. They note its egotistical emphasis and wonder how it can possibly be combined with the teachings of Jesus— whose life reflected humble service. While far too many Christians fail to see the contradiction! It is reminiscent of 2 Timothy 4:3, where Paul warned that a time would come when Christians would neglect sound teaching, and surround themselves with teachers who cater to their desires, telling them what they want to hear.

In the creative book *The Screwtape Letters* by C.S. Lewis, an experienced devil gives advice to an inexperienced devil on how to tempt humans. One piece of advice is to confuse humans about what true humility is by making them think it is having a low opinion of yourself. That is not true humility; true humility is self-forgetfulness. This was indeed a sneaky tactic by these devils, to create pride by discrediting its opposite. The positive thinking mentality exploited this route of temptation. It is my hope that content in several coming chapters of this book will bring increasing clarity about Christian humility.

Spiritual Pride

A dangerous and insidious type of pride is the pride of self-righteousness. We can drift into varying degrees of self-satisfaction in our Christian life. Ruth Tucker, in a book entitled *Walking Away From Faith*, graciously considers the issue of Christians who reject their faith. Some of these former believers find their post-faith life a hopeless struggle, while others find it a huge improvement. In the latter category, one of these former believers stated:

> The greatest benefit I discovered was the disappearance of a spiritual barrier for me between people. When I had strong religion…I was in a 'spiritually superior state.' Now I see Christians just as people with a mistaken belief…I now see us all as vulnerable human beings full of hopes and fears and psychological tangle.[25]

I see this as a woeful commentary for us as believers. Shouldn't that quote be reversed? Our faith should make us humble, vulnerable, and cause us to simply see people as people. It can't be denied that believers too often come across in a spiritually superior state, and we mete out judgment and condescension rather than grace.

The classic passage on spiritual pride is the parable told by Jesus in Luke 18:9-14 that features a Pharisee and a tax collector. It begins with the direct statement (verse 9) that Jesus told this parable as a message "to some who were confident of their own righteousness and looked down on everyone else." Pharisees were a respected

Jewish sect known for their piety and obedience to God's laws. Tax collectors, on the other hand, had a bad reputation among the Jews. They were typically dishonest and extorted excessive money from the people. Since they collaborated with the Romans, they were also thought of as traitors. In this parable, both men pray. The Pharisee prays by thanking God that he is not like other men in committing certain sins and reminds God that he has fasted and tithed. The goodness we think we possess can distance us from God, hindering our ability to see how much we need him.

> Our confidence should not be in our righteousness, but in Christ's righteousness.

In contrast, the tax collector was acutely aware of his sinfulness and simply pleaded for mercy as a sinner. Note that the Pharisee compared himself to other people. We will always be able to find people who are worse than we are, thus boosting our sense of moral success. The tax collector did not compare himself to others. Jerry Bridges points out that it is even more poignant in the original Greek, as the statement of the tax collector actually reads "God be merciful to me *the* sinner" rather than *a* sinner.[26] He was the sinner, standing alone before God, and he realized in comparison to God he fell desperately short.

The parable ends with a clear statement that it was the tax collector who went home right with God because of his humility. This is a dire warning for us as practicing Christians. There is at least some Pharisee in all of us, but many of us fail to see it. Our confidence should not be in our righteousness, but in Christ's righteousness. Pride lurks around the corner, and its danger is greater and nearer than we think.

Perils of Too Much Positive Thinking

I read a motivational book published in recent times by a well-known and successful Christian pastor. This and other similar titles by him continue to sell. Throughout the entire book, self-affirmation was the primary emphasis with the goal of our success in life or achieving our destiny. Continually it offered ways to encourage yourself personally by concentrating on your talents and capabilities. Through methods such as meditation, self-talk, or repeating certain statements each morning, we are to positively affirm ourselves at every opportunity. The book said we should *never* speak a critical word against ourselves.

How, may I ask, is this helpful? Like the danger of a recovering alcoholic hanging out in a bar, it hardly seems wise to immerse ourselves in nothing but positive thinking mantra. We already have a proclivity to self-exaltation without an approach that further encourages it. A wise friend of mine once noted that there is a fine line between confidence and pride. A healthy confidence is certainly good and not sinful, but the lopsided emphasis of this book is fertile soil for growing pride and self-delusion.

Two chapters of this book were about developing a sensitive conscience, heeding it, and dealing with root issues by not making excuses for your bad behavior. I agree with that, and it redeemed the book a little. Nevertheless, even those chapters were bathed in affirmative language, and the book's overall approach makes it challenging to perceive your sin. When you do nothing but positively affirm yourself, how will it help you face your sin?

Proverbs 16:18 is well known by many people and warns us that "pride goes before destruction, a haughty spirit before a fall." The apostle Paul echoes something similar in 1 Corinthians 10:12 when he says "If you think you are standing firm, be careful that you don't fall!" Please note that the alternative to positive thinking is not negative thinking. Negative thinking is just as delusional as unquestioned positive thinking. The point is that *too much* positive thinking lowers our awareness and blinds us to potential problems. Ouch, we trip and fall. In other words, there is safety in humility.

In a similar fashion, the apostle Peter wisely stated in 1 Peter 5:8, "Be alert and of sober mind. Your enemy the devil prowls around like a roaring lion looking for someone to devour." Sober? The first thing that may come to your mind is that a person is not under the influence of alcohol, but the word sober more traditionally referred to a sensible frame of mind. It is not about being positive or negative, but about having a healthy self-suspicion and being humble enough to admit you are not above reproach. We need to be alert, and regard with caution anything that lowers our awareness to temptation and sin. If biblical characters such as Abraham, Moses, David, and Peter stumbled in sin—it can happen to us too.

> There is safety in humility.

Secular sociology and psychology can point us to some of the problems inherent in an approach that goes overboard affirming our abilities and potential. As the title of one article proclaims: "Confidence is Good; Overconfidence, Not So Much."[27] We are already naturally prone to overestimate ourselves. It is referred to as the overconfidence phenomenon or effect. Studies done by psychologists show that we have a cognitive bias to be more confident than correct when asked questions. We are surer of our answers and abilities than we should be. Social science research also shows that most people think they are better than others. They perceive themselves as possessing a higher level of ethical traits than the typical person. One polling expert notes: "It's the great contradiction: the average person thinks he is a better person than the average person."[28]

An article from 2014 in *The New Yorker* was entitled "The Powerlessness of Positive Thinking," and it highlighted recent studies indicating that excessive positive thinking can decrease your chance of success. It is quoted that:

> Ceaseless optimism about the future only makes for a greater shock when things go wrong; by fighting to maintain only positive beliefs about the future, the positive thinker ends up being less prepared, and more acutely distressed, when things eventually happen that he can't persuade himself to believe are good.[29]

This is similar to the biblical warnings highlighted from Proverbs and from the apostles Paul and Peter. We need to be prepared and not have a blindly optimistic outlook. Despite increased consideration of the pitfalls of positive thinking, the critique is not popular as it goes against the general mindset of our culture. At some point in the distant or perhaps not-so-distant future, I think historians will look back with puzzlement at how a positive thinking and self-affirmation mentality took over our nation. It was like pouring gasoline on a fire.

While some sins can be overcome, I think pride is a sin that we will never completely conquer in this life. That doesn't mean we give up hope. That doesn't mean we can't mature spiritually and grow in the likeness of our humble Savior. But denial is never effective, and until we can humbly admit our weakness we will never improve. The positive thinking culture that surrounds us on nearly every side has lulled us to sleep. We need to wake up from our slumber.

Questions for Reflection and Discussion

1. Had you ever thought of God as humble before reading this chapter? Humility is rarely emphasized as a characteristic of God. Why do you think this is the case?

2. Pride is the sin we are most likely to overlook in ourselves. How has this chapter heightened your awareness of its perils?

3. One way to detect pride in ourselves is to consider how we respond to criticism. Are we easily offended? Resentful? Defensive? Pray for humility to graciously accept critique.

4. Why is self-righteousness so repugnant?

We Interrupt This Book
for an Intermission

Are you worried this book is just going to be negative about being positive? Can we ever be positive or encourage others? Doesn't the Bible teach that our thought life is important? This brief "intermission" will clarify potential concerns or misunderstandings before the book continues...

As touched on in the previous chapter, the alternative to positive thinking is not negative thinking! Instead of wearing rose-colored glasses or black-colored glasses, we need to wear *clear* glasses. As Christians, we need optimism about the future which is tempered by the reality of the doctrine of original sin. That is the ultimate point that should become clear by the end of the book.

There is also no argument that our thought life is important and does affect us. In Philippians 4:8, we are encouraged as believers to think about things that are true, noble, right, pure, lovely, admirable, excellent, and praiseworthy. Regarding what is true, our Lord Jesus Christ proclaimed himself to be the truth. His sacrificial life, death, and resurrection should be a major focus of our thoughts. Indeed, Colossians 3:1-2 says to fix our hearts and minds on Jesus and on things above—not on earthly things. The Bible also encourages us to meditate upon God's laws and commandments (Joshua 1:8; Psalm 119) which are personified in the life of Christ. Is our thought life Christ-focused and Christ-honoring? Paul urges us to take our thoughts captive in obedience to Christ (2 Corinthians 10:5).

Certainly we are told to be transformed by the renewing of our minds (Romans 12:2). What we think about can put us on the right or wrong path in life, so in this aspect, our thoughts can affect our future.

These things, however, are distinctly different from what positive thinking espouses. Christianity cannot be built around an optimistic motivational philosophy because the two belief systems are at odds with each other. One begins with God, and the other begins with self. In contrast to fixing our thoughts on Jesus, positive thinking turns us inward. It's about us, our goals or desires, and affirming ourselves. It is an anti-gospel of self-absorption. I hardly think that Philippians 4:8's encouragement to think about things that are lovely and excellent is inferring that we should be thinking *of ourselves* as lovely and excellent!

As believers, we may have admirable goals to serve God, but the positive thinking paradigm puts a narcissistic spin on it. It ends up about *us* doing great things *for* God, rather than about *God* doing great things *through* us. Don't miss the subtle but significant difference there. In Colossians 1:9-14, you can read a powerful prayer by Paul for the Colossian Christians. If you observantly read the passage, what really stands out is the focus on God. Although Paul is praying for people, it is God's knowledge and power that is paramount. It is not about the Colossian's capabilities, minds, or their ability to do great things for God. Rather, Paul prays that God will fill them—and out of that fullness from God—the Colossians would bear God's fruit in their lives.

> True power is found in a Christ-centered life.

True power is found in a Christ-centered life. I appreciate how *The Message* words 1 Corinthians 10:11-12, "Don't be so naive and self-confident...You could fall flat on your face as easily as anyone else. Forget about self-confidence; it's useless. Cultivate God-confidence." Our goal should not be self-confidence, but confidence in Christ and what Christ can do in our life.

Be sure not to miss that it is *the power of* positive thinking. To some extent, either ambiguously or explicitly, the confidence is placed in the thinking. The object of our faith can cease to be God. Our thoughts are in essence elevated to a god-like status with the capability of yielding power or bringing change. Additionally, let us not forget that as sinful human beings our thoughts can deceive us. Our faith should not be in the power of our thoughts but in the power of God. Ephesians 3:20-21 states: "Now to him who is able to do immeasurably more than all we ask or imagine, *according to his power that is at work within us*, to him be glory in the church and in Christ Jesus throughout all generations, for ever and ever! Amen" (emphasis added). Power in the Scripture is linked with God, the gospel, or Jesus Christ: Romans 1:16; 2 Peter 1:2-3; 1 Corinthians 1:18, 24; 2 Corinthians 4:7.

Finally, critiquing positive thinking does not suggest that we should not encourage others. We simply need to consider *how* we are doing it. Are we puffing people up or anchoring them in Christ? The prayer in Colossians 1:9-14 is an ideal example of a God-centered way to encourage each other through prayer. The verses preceding it (verses 3-8) provide another illustration. Paul lets the Colossians know that he heard good things about them. They had faith in Christ and a love for other people. We should not hesitate to point out the good in others or let them know when we have heard a good report. However, Paul does not let them lose sight of Jesus. He states that their faith and love is evidence that the gospel is bearing fruit in their lives and that they truly understood God's grace. Everything flows from what God did for them through our Lord Jesus Christ. We need to offer Christ-centered encouragement instead of self-centered encouragement. With those clarifications, let's continue with this book.

Chapter 3

The Damage Report is Extensive

If we are not growing in awareness of our personal sin and
depravity and our profound need for grace…then we are not
growing closer to a holy God. We are growing closer to spiritual
narcissism. Blindness and denial to personal sin is the fertile
soil in which idolatry, heresy, and narcissism grows. The love
and grace of Jesus Christ radically transforms the ones who
understand how profoundly they need him. —Carole Chaput

Sin. Not a popular topic. Yet sin needs to be taken seriously and
not swept under the carpet. It is our sin that brought Jesus to this
world for us. It is our sin that nailed Jesus to the cross. As the apostle
Peter states in 1 Peter 3:18, "For Christ also suffered once for sins,
the righteous for the unrighteous, to bring you to God." Anything
that makes light of sin makes light of the redemptive work of our
Lord Jesus Christ.

It is apparent that we need a remedial course on sin. Throughout
the Bible, humans are portrayed as prone to think too highly of
themselves, so this weakness is nothing new. The church, for the
most part, has maintained its belief in original sin, and a light view
of sin has generally not been the problem. However, during the

Enlightenment, things changed and there have been a number of onslaughts against sin. The church was no longer the source of authority in people's lives. Instead, an inward source—whether the mind or common sense—gained prominence. The individual was elevated, and this influenced the past several centuries of history including Christianity.

For example, there was the rise of Liberal Protestantism in the eighteenth and nineteenth centuries. Among other things, Liberal Protestantism took an optimistic view of human abilities, and a consciousness of sin was lost. The gulf between humanity and God was minimized, and in its wake, the cross and the need for salvation was minimized as well. We need to learn from the past. History has a way of repeating itself, but maybe it wouldn't quite so often if we actually paid attention.

It doesn't seem surprising that New Thought ideas began to develop not long after this time period. In essence, New Thought deified humanity and humanized God. Jones and Woodbridge summarize New Thought literature by stating that it "reveals a human-centered philosophy that asserts that people are intrinsically good, spiritual beings, with the potential for godlike—if not divine—status."[30] In the history of New Thought presented in chapter 1, several Protestant ministers or theologians were mentioned. It should be evident that New Thought philosophies and Christianity contradict each other. They don't blend, yet they were blended. It should serve as a warning that anyone, including a minister, can get pulled into false teaching, and the dilution of Christianity has far reaching effects.

> The dilution of Christianity has far reaching effects.

There are multiple perils caused by taking a light view of sin. It can induce false views of God and lead to doctrinal errors. If you mess up the problem (sin), you mess up the solution (Christ and his great salvation). We are not sinners because we sin. We sin because we are sinners. Read those two sentences again as they make an important distinction. The opening chapters of Romans expound on the sinfulness of humanity. No one is exempt. Romans 3:23 states "For all have sinned and fall short of the glory of God." All means all. Some people are offended that a baby is considered sinful according to orthodox Christian doctrine. A baby, in one sense, is innocent. Yet as a baby grows, you do not have to teach the baby to be bad. They know how to be bad. "No!" may be one of the first words uttered by an infant. Because we are all born sinners theologians refer to this as original sin. We have a "hereditary" sinfulness passed on to us from Adam (Romans 5:12).

When Adam and Eve rebelled in Genesis chapter 3, humanity and earth alike were judged or cursed by sin. Every aspect of our humanity was corrupted: our physical bodies, our hearts, and our minds. Jeremiah 17:9 reminds us that our hearts are deceitful. Romans 12:2 tells believers to be transformed by the renewing of their minds. Our minds have been corrupted by sin and need renewal. The tense of the word renewing in the verse indicates an ongoing process. Sin affects our thinking, and we should be cautious of any scheme that elevates our thoughts.

Don't Be Naïve About Sin

Many people, Christian and non-Christian alike, have problems with the doctrine of original sin and human depravity. The pervasive effect of positive thinking does not make it any easier to face up to the reality of our innate sin. Many people insist that humanity is really good at heart even though we sometimes do bad things. Yes, of course, people can do good things. Many of us are not nearly as bad as we could be, but the fact remains that our basic nature is sinful. G.K. Chesterton is often remembered for his remark in his book *Orthodoxy* that "Certain new theologians dispute original sin, which is the only part of Christian theology that can really be proved."[31] He saw it as the one doctrine that could actually be verified by the observation of human behavior and history.

Some Christians who *say* that they believe in human sinfulness do not *act* as though they believe in it. There is a disconnect between theory and reality. Some are simply naïve about human nature and consequently disillusioned by the sin they see around them. They may fail to properly guide their children because they naively think their children incapable of certain sinful behaviors. "My child would *never* do that." Really? Never? Surprise, they did it. I like watching true-crime documentary type television shows. It seems common to hear a relative or friend defend the accused saying, "He (or she) could *never* _____." (Fill in the blank with the crime of your choice.) Really? Never? Given the right circumstances, right frustrations, and right provocations I think we are all capable of things worse than we have ever imagined. I half-jokingly told my husband that if he was accused of a crime, and I was asked if he was at least capable of it, I'd have to say yes. He hopes he is never falsely accused because my opinion would not help his case!

This is not intended to make us pessimistic and look upon others with deep suspicion all the time. In fact, the famous description of love in 1 Corinthians 13 says that love always trusts. Does that mean we are supposed to be gullible? I don't think so. All human beings are made in the image of God, and reflections of God and his goodness can be seen in everyone. We need to remember that we are all noble ruins. As Mark McMinn states,

> We are ruined by the effects of sin; we see our brokenness in every aspect of the created order. The damage report is extensive. Yet we are noble, made in God's image and graciously deemed worthy of redemption.[32]

How does this relate to love always trusts? We need a realistic view of human nature rather than a pessimistic or optimistic one. Love is not naïve, and people are certainly capable of terrible acts, but love gives the benefit of the doubt or avoids unnecessary suspicion.

However, an accurate understanding of human sinfulness is imperative. In his book on humanity and sin, Robert Pyne suggests that our beliefs about human nature and the role of grace determine the course of our theology like a rudder on a boat. He explains:

> The issue of human ability shapes our expectations for individual morality, social reformation, and spiritual regeneration. It affects the methods we employ in evangelism, discipleship, preaching, and teaching.[33]

I also appreciate how Pyne remarks that you will be less likely to be disillusioned when you don't have too many illusions from which to be "dissed!" Some feel that focusing on human sinfulness will lead to hopelessness, despair, and self-loathing. While it could, I definitely do not think this will be the case *when there is also a focus on Jesus Christ.* A realistic view of our depravity should instead lead us to a life of watchfulness, compassion, faithfulness, and prayer. I have personally found that a realistic understanding of my utter sinfulness makes me more amazed and appreciative of God's grace and mercy through Christ. It motivates me to live a life where I don't presume upon it. Keeping our sinfulness before us can keep us from sin. It is when we overestimate our own goodness and fail to consider our weakness that we are prone to wander into sin.

Don't Take Sin Lightly

Sin can be taken lightly in many ways including narrowing its definition. What if you sinned but it was not willful, intentional, or premeditated? What if you sinned but weren't aware of it? Certain theological traditions can make distinctions here, at least historically. I was part of an evangelical group that claimed to take sin seriously. In a certain way they did as holy living was a prime theme of their teaching and doctrine. Encouraging Christians to live holy lives is certainly a good thing. However, they also taught it was possible to reach a higher level of Christian life where you could go days, weeks, or months without committing sin. By the way, I did not believe this even though I was a part of this group for years. I believe I sin every day. Every single day. As you can imagine, this type of admission was not well received. You were not living up to the standard of the Christian life, or you were setting yourself up for failure by your pessimistic expectation to sin.

Do you wonder how it is possible to go days or weeks without sinning? It is possible if you narrow the definition of sin to only include willful sin or sin that you are explicitly aware of committing. It is true that we may sometimes sin non-willfully or without intention, but it is still sin regardless. Maybe our motive was not vicious, but the sin could have still hurt someone and it still violated God's perfection. Even if you do accept a distinction about what qualifies as sin, I worry about the subjective aspect. Is the line between willful and non-willful really that clear cut? It seems easy for pretense or rationalization to take place, and that is not a good path to begin walking down.

It also places an unhealthy spotlight on self. If you say you can go days, weeks, or months without sinning, that sounds like you are keeping record on a calendar. I'm reminded of one of those signs at a construction site: "Don't take chances with your safety. ____ days without an accident." How many days since you sinned? If you think you can go extended periods of time without sinning, it is an easy slide into pride and self-deception. Therefore, you will end up in sin anyways.

Rationalizing sin is nothing new. We are all guilty of it in one way or another. It has gone on since Adam and Eve. Remember the blame game about eating the apple? We look for ways to avoid admitting and taking responsibility for our actions by calling sin a mistake or an accident. We are clever spiritual spin doctors who sanctify our sin by claiming a valid reason for why we did it. But we must honestly name our sin for what it is in God's sight regardless of the intent or lack of intent behind it.

> We are clever spiritual spin doctors who sanctify our sin.

It is indeed possible to commit sin and be ignorant of it. Does that make you innocent? Maybe this is something you have never considered before. Sin is not the knowledge of sinning, and a whole world of sin lies just beneath the surface. In Psalm 19:12, David says, "But who can discern their own errors? Forgive my hidden faults." If something is not sin, we do not need forgiveness for it. These hidden faults were still sin regardless of a lack of cognizance. David would have been familiar with passages in Leviticus 4 and 5 where Israel was taught that there were sins of ignorance that needed atonement anyway. I've been a Christian over thirty years now, and at times I've looked back and my eyes were opened about past sinful behavior. At that time in the past, I was completely blinded to the sin. Hebrews 3:13 refers to the "deceitfulness of sin." Sin itself can trick us, blur our spiritual vision, and dull our conscience. We can simply fail to see the sin in our life.

My years in the aforementioned group taught me some valuable lessons. I often appreciated the optimistic outlook, yet it did not seem successful when the rubber hit the road. Interestingly, leaders within this tradition have recently admitted as much. In the book *Be Holy* from 2008, one contributor candidly states that holiness preaching was too often overstated and under-lived, and many did not experience the levels of godliness preached and expected.[34] I was encouraged by the more balanced perspective that is now being presented by those from within this tradition.

Sin has appalling force and destructive power all on its own without our emboldening it. In explaining why he decided to write his book on sin, Cornelius Plantinga Jr. said there was a loss of consciousness of sin in society. He goes on to state:

> Self-deception about our sin is a narcotic, a tranquilizing and disorienting suppression of our spiritual nervous system. What's devastating about it is that when we lack an ear for wrong notes in our lives, we cannot play right ones or even recognize them in the performances of others.[35]

We must be brutally honest about our sin and not evade it, rationalize it, or re-define it to make it seem less serious. If you deny a problem, nothing can be done about it; admit to it, and there is a possibility of solution. The truth can hurt, but the truth can also set us free (John 8:31-36; Romans 8:1-2).

Don't Evade Your Sin

In Romans 14:23 it says "everything that does not come from faith is sin." This certainly broadens the definition of sin. It is from a section in Romans where "questionable" matters are being considered that might be appropriate for one believer but not another. If you have doubts about whether a certain behavior is appropriate for you, then you should not do it. To violate your conscience is a sin. Another convicting verse is found in James 4:17, which states "If anyone, then, knows the good they ought to do and doesn't do it, it is sin for them." Many times I knew I could have done a good deed but failed to do so due to laziness, forgetfulness, or other excuses.

The teachings of Jesus make it even more difficult to evade our sin. Motives and thoughts, not actions alone, make us guilty. For example, Jesus condemned anger and lust as vehemently as he did murder and adultery (Matthew 5:21-22, 27-28). We could possibly go days at a time without any outward sins of action, but to also remain pure in thoughts and motives is nearly impossible.

Even the good we do is not likely pure. A statement attributed to C.H. Spurgeon is convicting in this regard:

> The saints are sinners still. Our best tears need to be wept over, the strongest faith is mixed with unbelief, our most flaming love is cold compared with what Jesus deserves, and our intensest zeal still lacks the full fervor which the bleeding wounds and pierced heart of the crucified might claim at our hands. Our best things need a sin offering, or they would condemn us.

Let's face it; even our best deeds are done for a combination of good and not-so-good reasons. Our attitude may be halfhearted. The Scripture says in Luke 10:27 that we are to love God with our *whole* heart, soul, strength, and mind. If we are honest, God is only getting part of us. We love him well with one aspect of our being but not with another.

Ulterior motives abound, and we may do the right thing because we are seeking approval or other benefits. Personal self-interest is mixed up with most things we do. Speaking of the self, A.W. Tozer refers to the "hyphenated sins of the human spirit" such as self-righteousness, self-love, self-pity, self-confidence, self-sufficiency, self-admiration, and others. In regards to these, Tozer says:

> They are not something we do, they are something
> we are, and therein lies both their subtlety and their
> power…They dwell too deep within us and are too
> much a part of our natures to come to our attention
> till the light of God is focused upon them. [36]

While the positive thinking movement certainly did not create this problem of self-absorption, it surely exacerbated it and further blinds our ability to realize it.

I heard a pastor make the point that we can appear to be obeying God when in fact we are only doing things that we wanted to do anyway. Depending on our personalities, certain good behaviors may just come naturally to us, and certain sins may never be a weakness for us. We can't take credit or "claim victory" for these things, and it is another way to delude ourselves, focus on our own righteousness, and overlook sin in our life. The behaviors that are more difficult for us to change are precisely the ones that the Spirit wants to transform in us. God may want to stretch us by leading us outside of our comfort zone to do something we do not want to do. Many of us are stubborn and hard-headed just like the Israelites of old.

Another concern, particularly in recent evangelicalism, is we have defined sin in its more obvious or tangible forms such as sexual immorality, murder, stealing, drunkenness, and the like. Phew, we've not done any of those things! Meanwhile we forget about less blatant sins, socially acceptable sins, or sins that can hide within us such as: resentment, an unforgiving spirit, ingratitude, discontent, bitterness, gossip, impatience, envy, and rudeness. While some of these things may hide, they can nonetheless be destructive to our souls.

An unbelieving friend of mine once told me that the "socially acceptable" sins of the evangelical Christians caused more hurt to other people than the "big sins" the evangelicals like to point their fingers at in judgment. Romans chapter 1 has an extensive list of sins, yet it is typically the sexual sin that gets the attention. We miss the point. The list is not selective but inclusive and encompassing. Everyone should find they are guilty of something on the list. As Robert Pyne summarizes about this passage:

> The apostle's purpose…was not to highlight particular evils and single out certain persons for condemnation, but to reject summarily all kinds of evils and to include all persons in the need for salvation.[37]

The Hope of the Gospel

It seems quite evident that we sin every single day. Are you wondering what the point is exactly? Am I trying to make people feel depressed? Like failures? Discouraged? Am I promoting negative thinking? Does it appear that I am encouraging sin by presenting it as inevitable? No, to all those things. Sin is inevitable, and we simply need to face the truth. Denial or avoidance is not effective when dealing with any type of problem. We shouldn't be afraid or hesitant to admit our sin. After all, that is what the gospel is all about, isn't it? Romans 5:6-8 states:

> You see, at just the right time, when we were still powerless, Christ died for the ungodly. Very rarely will anyone die for a righteous person, though for a good person someone might possibly dare to die.

> But God demonstrates his own love for us in this:
> While we were still sinners, Christ died for us.

Christ died for the powerless, ungodly, and sinful. That describes you and me! This should give us a tremendous sense of relief and hope. The bad news of our sinfulness points us to the good news of salvation found in Christ. Don't we deeply appreciate the people in our lives that have seen us at our worst yet love us? As Brennan Manning states, "Getting honest with ourselves does not make us unacceptable to God. It does not distance us from God, but draws us to him—as nothing else can—and opens us anew to the flow of grace."[38] Although our sin separates us from God, and that is why we need a Savior, our sin does not create a barricade *in our approach* to him. God knew the worst about humanity and loved us anyway by sending Jesus, the Son, to sacrifice his life for our sin. What marvelous love! No one is beyond redemption.

> Don't lose sight of Jesus and why you need him!

At this point you could be thinking, "but I'm already a Christian…I already accepted the gospel…I'm living the Christian life now." Does that mean you no longer need the gospel? Sin is why you needed the gospel, and sin is why you continue to need the gospel. We are saved by grace through faith, but we are to continue living by grace through faith. If you no longer perceive yourself as sinful, the gospel has been marginalized in your life. J.I. Packer said, "The traveler through the Bible landscape misses his way as soon as he loses sight of the hill called Calvary."[39] No matter where we are in our spiritual journey, we still need the gospel. Paul continued to preach it even to the believers, as he says in 1 Corinthians 15:1-4:

> Now, brothers and sisters, I want to **remind you**
> of the gospel I preached to you, which you received

and on which you have taken **your stand**. By this gospel you are saved, if you **hold firmly** to the word I preached to you. Otherwise, you have believed in vain. For what I received I passed on to you as of **first importance**: that Christ died for our sins according to the Scriptures, that he was buried, that he was raised on the third day according to the Scriptures [emphasis added].

The Corinthians were standing on the gospel, which means it is the foundation of their faith, and they were to keep holding onto the gospel. Paul was now reminding them of the gospel. *Apparently the gospel is pretty important.* Don't lose sight of Jesus and why you need him! If you have never come to a personal saving knowledge of the Lord Jesus Christ, I urge you to trust him today.

Questions for Reflection and Discussion

1. Consider the sections of the chapter. Has your weakness been to be naïve about sin? Take sin lightly? Evade your sin?
2. A realistic view of our sinfulness should lead to a life of watchfulness, compassion, faithfulness, and prayer. Consider compassion. How should it make us more compassionate?
3. "Sin is inevitable." How might you respond to the concern that this standpoint will only encourage sin?
4. How does having a greater sense of your sin give you a greater appreciation for God's salvation through Christ?

Chapter 4

The Already but Not Yet

Over-realized eschatology promises heaven on earth, as though we have already received all of God's promises in the present world. —Thomas Schreiner & Ardel Caneday

This life was not intended to be the place of our perfection, but the preparation for it. —Richard Baxter

The followers of Jesus are realists, not Utopians...the perfect society...awaits the return of Jesus. —John Stott

Due to the perils of positive thinking and pride, must we neglect the positive verses in the Bible? As Christians, are we supposed to walk around thinking of ourselves as pathetic sinners all the time? What about Bible verses which refer to believers as saints, new creations, and victors? God calls us to be holy people; is he calling us to be something we can't be? Can't we make progress in the Christian life? These questions and more will be addressed in the next several chapters.

Positive thinking has clouded our perceptions of life in this world. A large part of the problem is that we've lost sight of where we are in the story of redemption. The Bible isn't just a random collection of stories. It is telling the "one" story of God's plan for this world, and all of history is moving towards the climactic conclusion. The big plan or overarching theme of the Bible could be summarized this way:

Creation of the World (Genesis 1-2)
↓
The Fall of Humanity into Sin (Genesis 3)
↓
The Cross of Christ and his Resurrection (Gospels)
↓
New Heaven and Earth at Christ's Return (Revelation 21-22)

Genesis chapters 1 and 2 and Revelation chapters 21 and 22 can be thought of as "bookends" for the big story of redemption. The world was once perfect and will once again be perfect. In Genesis 3 humanity fell into sin, but immediately Genesis 3:15 offered a hint of God's plan to provide a way of redemption. The redeemer would be Jesus Christ. Today we live in a time of overlap. It is *after* Christ's first coming, and yet it is *before* Christ's second coming.

At the cross of Christ, the future invaded the present but in a limited sense. Our future hopes were initiated, but they will not reach their fullness or completion until the return of Christ. Steve Estes and Joni Eareckson Tada state it this way in a book they co-authored on why there is suffering in this world:

> Yes, Jesus took up our diseases (Isaiah 53:4). His cross is our ship to heaven; his miracles give us glimpses of paradise; he ladles out foretastes of bliss by a thousand blessings large and small. But they are all just that— glimpses, foretastes. We're not in heaven yet.[40]

All of salvation's blessings are not to be experienced now, and we are not immune to the repercussions of life in a fallen world that is awaiting the final redemption. We will experience sickness, tragedy, natural disasters, broken relationships, and other consequences of humanity's fall into sin as we go through this life. Yet we have hope. We know that death, the final enemy, was defeated by the death and resurrection of Jesus (1 Corinthians 15).

You likely recognized the name of Joni Eareckson Tada, who realizes more than some of us the limitations of life in the present time. Joni and her family prayed for healing but it never came, and Joni has spent her life as a quadriplegic confined to a wheelchair. Despite this, Joni is a woman of tremendous joy and hope who has described her wheelchair as the prison God used to set her spirit free. The pragmatic approach of positive thinking leads us to think faith must always "work" or show tangible results in the here and now. But in all reality, faith may not always work this side of eternity, and some broken things may not be whole until the final redemption. Oh how we long for that day! That ache we sometimes have that things are not quite right in this world is the seed of eternity in our hearts.

> All of salvation's blessings are not to be experienced now.

We are supposed to feel a bit restless and disappointed in this life. It is not a flaw in our faith; it is woven into the very substance of it. Hebrews 11:1 reminds us that "faith is confidence in what we hope for and assurance about what we do not see." There is a new and better world coming to which we can look with confidence.

Likewise, Paul said in 2 Corinthians 4:18 that we should "fix our eyes not on what is seen, but on what is unseen, since what is seen is temporary, but what is unseen is eternal." Earth matters, and what we do in the here and now can impact eternity, but our eyes should ultimately be fixed on the unseen. An eternal perspective helped Paul through difficulties in life, as he proclaimed in verses

8-9 of the same chapter that they were "hard pressed on every side, but not crushed; perplexed, but not in despair; persecuted, but not abandoned; struck down, but not destroyed." Hard pressed? Struck down? This does not sound like a vision of positive thinking and success! Nevertheless, Paul was a faithful servant of Jesus, and Godly success may look different than worldly success.

Paul further declared in Philippians 3:10: "I want to know Christ—yes, to know the power of his resurrection and participation in his sufferings, becoming like him in his death." Do you see the paradoxical connection between power and suffering? Remember how Satan tempted Jesus in the wilderness in Luke chapter four. In one temptation, Satan offered Jesus authority and splendor if Jesus would only worship him. There is danger in trying to impose the future on the present before the proper time. Satan offered Jesus glory without the cross, but the cross was a critical part of God's plan. Glory is coming but we can't short circuit the way there.

One Christian book from a positive thinking perspective portrays Jesus as our coach who wants us to win in every area of life. However, it is Satan who continues to tempt by shifting the focus to our success and glory in this life. Jesus responded to his temptation with a reference from Deuteronomy: "Worship the Lord your God and serve him only." In the original context, Moses was warning the people about their attitude when they reached the Promised Land. Their temptation would be to forget God and be consumed by other gods and distractions in the land. Satan's promises are always deceitful and distract us from what matters.

Christian Living: Progress not Perfection

How does this relate to the questions at the beginning of the chapter? When it comes to living the Christian life, there is a tendency to confuse life in the present with how it will be in the future. We take promises or expectations that will reach their *fullness* when Christ returns and falsely expect them to be *fully* possible now. In theological terminology, this is called over-realized eschatology or triumphalism. There are limits to our success in the present time. This does not mean we are defeated! The gospel does have transformative power; we do make progress in our spiritual life and grow in the likeness of Jesus, but we need reasonable expectations. The world is not perfect yet, and we cannot be perfect yet either. It is progress, not perfection.

The Bible, of course, refers to Christians in many positive ways: we are saints, new creations, and victors. We are told to be perfect as our heavenly Father is perfect (Matthew 5:48) and to be holy as God is holy (1 Peter 1:16). Yet there must be some type of tension here. This is not lowering the bar. By all means we should aim high, and God should be the standard, but we obviously cannot be as perfect or as holy as God. We have the promised Holy Spirit, but Ephesians 1:13-14 refers to the Holy Spirit as "a deposit guaranteeing our inheritance" which we will receive on the future day of redemption. The Holy Spirit is a deposit? One commentator explains: "In essence, the 'deposit' of the Holy Spirit is a little bit of heaven in believers' lives with a guarantee of much more to come."[41] Praise God that more is to come!

We will end up with distorted theology if we attempt to make certain Bible verses be completely true and possible in the present age. These distorted teachings can create more problems than they were intended to resolve. We are not *completely* new creations. If we are, the Christian faith is quite disappointing because we still struggle with sin and the troubles of life in a fallen world. I demand a refund if this is life in its fullness as a new creation! But even when we reach our future eternal home, we will still be creatures, and God will remain the Creator.

Salvation: Past, Present, and Future

There is an "already but not yet" aspect of our salvation that often seems overlooked. Too often we think of our salvation as primarily something in the past. Particularly as evangelicals, we tend to look back to a moment when we accepted Christ and made a decision to follow him. However, our salvation is not only a past reality; it is also our future destiny. We were saved in the past, but we are also being saved as we live out our faith now, and one day in the future our salvation will be complete. Our salvation is past, present, and future.

Romans 13:11 says that "our salvation is nearer now than when we first believed." We have not arrived, but are on our way. The book of Hebrews has a tremendous future focus. Hebrews 9:28 says that Christ came the first time to sacrifice himself for our sin, and "he will appear a second time, not to bear sin, but to bring salvation to those who are waiting for him." We have salvation, yet it is also a future event.

We "have redemption" (Colossians 1:14), and we are adopted into God's family and can call God our Father (Romans 8:15), yet we also "groan inwardly as we wait eagerly" for our adoption and redemption in the future (Romans 8:23). The New Testament is filled with this tension, revealing the "already but not yet" aspect of our salvation that needs to be maintained as we live our Christian life. Overstating either side of the issue is not helpful. If asked if you are saved, the correct biblical answer would technically be yes and no, as John Stott summarizes:

> Yes, in the sense that by the sheer grace and mercy of God through the death of Jesus Christ my Savior he has forgiven my sins, justified me and reconciled me to himself. But, no, in the sense that I still live in a fallen world and have a corruptible body, and

I am longing for my salvation to be brought to its triumphant completion.[42]

If we overemphasize the "already," we can end up with false delusions about our present abilities to triumph in the Christian life. We've also likely observed Christianity presented in an overly rosy fashion that accentuates the benefits of Christianity or portrays the Christian life as one where problems will melt away. When expectations and reality clash, this can lead to disappointment, disillusionment, or even rejection of faith. Christianity promised but did not deliver. Is it a farce?

A person could doubt their salvation because it is not working as well as they were led to believe possible. Do they need to be born again *again*? They pray a second (or third…) time to accept Christ as Savior as it did not seem to "take" the original time. They may end up on a spiritual treadmill of sorts, constantly looking for a spiritual secret that will bump them up to a higher level of Christian living—but never finding it. They could give up and use it as an excuse for sinful living or rationalize some of their sin to make it *appear* they are doing better than they are in reality.

Overstating the possibilities of life in the present age can feed our natural proclivity to self-deception and pride. Optimism can degenerate into a presumptuous attitude. It is all too easy for us to think we are something when we are not. As Romans 12:3 states, "Do not think of yourself more highly than you ought, but rather think of yourself with sober judgment."

However, overemphasizing the "not yet" can be problematic too. The "miserable sinner" emphasis can be overdone, hindering our ability to seek holiness of life. It can serve as an excuse for spiritual laziness and sinful behavior. It can also detract from our Lord's death and resurrection and all that was accomplished for us. Did he die to save us from our sin, or not? Are we living in light of Christ's work for us, or in light of our sinfulness? We can so stress our sin and the difficult side of the Christian life that we forget about the resurrection power of Jesus and the transforming work of the Holy Spirit in our life. An overemphasis on the "not yet" can also dash hope, and Christians are supposed to be people of tremendous hope! Biblical hope is a confident expectation of the future we have in Christ. Titus 2:11-14 tells us that:

> The grace of God has appeared that offers salvation to all people. It teaches us to say "No" to ungodliness and worldly passions, and to live self-controlled, upright and godly lives in this present age, while we wait for the blessed hope—the appearing of the glory of our great God and Savior, Jesus Christ, who gave himself for us to redeem us from all wickedness and to purify for himself a people that are his very own, eager to do what is good.

The grace of God and the hope of Christ's return should motivate us to be living for him, not produce spiritual sloth or apathy. If the later has occurred, we may need to return to the basics of the gospel. Are your eyes fixed on Jesus, or something else? A true life of godliness begins and grows with an awed adoration of the Lord Jesus Christ.

A true life of godliness begins and grows with an awed adoration of the Lord Jesus Christ.

Our focus should be on God, not on our success or failure. Either extreme of overstressing the "already" or the "not yet" can lead to an unhealthy focus on self. I once heard it said in regards to Hebrews 12:1-2 that we are told to run the race, not to keep score. If we stop running too often to keep score, we will hinder our ability to finish the race. We certainly should evaluate ourselves sometimes (2 Corinthians 13:5), but too much introspection can be counterproductive, even narcissistic, and lead us away from Christ.

Biblically Balanced Christianity

It is like we are on a seesaw, and it is critical to stay balanced in the middle. That can be hard to accomplish, as it is easy to tilt or slam down in one direction or the other. We are prone to isolate particular Bible verses, while ignoring others. We exalt one truth at the expense of another. Much of the Christian life requires maintaining a tension. As the subject of this book would indicate, tilting in the direction of the "already" is the predominant problem in our day. However, both dangers are before us, and we need to remember that the tension we experience is normal.

John Stott emphasizes the importance of biblical balance in his book entitled *The Contemporary Christian*. He explains that we are caught between the present and the future, and points out that Jesus regarded the kingdom of God as both a present phenomenon and a future expectation. Stott stresses we need a return to BBC or biblically balanced Christianity—a play on the letters of the British Broadcasting Corporation of his homeland. Stott sees the devil as the enemy of balance in the Christian life, and says the devil's "favorite pastime" is to upset our equilibrium.[43] The devil has unfortunately been successful, and lopsided Christianity is widespread. New Thought and the positive thinking movement took full advantage of this route of temptation. A proper grasp of this tension could resolve a variety of misunderstandings about the Christian life. We are not what we were before we came to Christ, yet we are not who we will be when we one day reach our eternal home. There is a saint and sinner in each of us, which leads to the next chapter.

Questions for Reflection and Discussion

1. How do we "fix our eyes" on things we cannot see?
   (2 Corinthians 4:18)
2. Worldly things can distract us from Christ and hinder an eternal perspective. Unfortunately, Christian things can do the same. Look with a discerning eye at the Christian books or messages that you typically expose yourself to. Are they distracting you by their emphasis on temporary things and success in this life?
3. Prayerfully consider your Christian life. Are there areas where you are imbalanced, having tipped into the "already" or the "not yet"? How can you return to a state of spiritual equilibrium?

Chapter 5

Simul Justus et Peccator

Any idea of getting beyond conflict, outward or inward,
in our pursuit of holiness in this world is an escapist dream
that can only have disillusioning and demoralizing effects
on us as waking experience daily disproves it. What we must
realize, rather, is that any real holiness in us will be under
hostile fire all the time, just as our Lord's was. —J.I. Packer

In light of the "already but not yet" in which we live, how should Christians perceive themselves? Should we think of ourselves as saints? as sinners? as saints *and* sinners? as saints who sin? A positive thinking mentality would have us focus on our status as saints. Maybe you have never thought about it before, or you think it is merely semantics. On the contrary, how we think of ourselves has significant implications for living the Christian life.

In 1 Timothy 1:15, the apostle Paul refers to himself as the worst of sinners. Interestingly, he uses the present tense—not the past tense—even though he is nearing the end of what can be considered an illustrious Christian life. How can this be? This makes some people uncomfortable, and one explanation is that Paul must be referring back to before he was a Christian and persecuting followers of Jesus. Along with this, it can be pointed out that Christians in the New Testament are not referred to as sinners. Instead they are labeled the elect, faithful brothers and sisters, children of God, and very frequently as saints.

Paul also refers to himself as the least of the apostles and as the least of the Lord's people (1 Corinthians 15:9; Ephesians 3:8). This fits right in with calling himself the worst of sinners. Does Paul need some remedial instruction on who we are in Christ? It would appear not, as the apostle Paul was a great teacher on these things! He wrote that we are new creations (2 Corinthians 5:17) who have been rescued from the dominion of darkness and brought into the kingdom of Jesus (Colossians 1:13). Is Paul confused? Is he suffering from a low self-image and in need of affirmation? Of course not!

Several explanations are helpful. Paul remembered his past, and this was humbling to him. He realized he could not boast about himself, but only in how Christ had shown him mercy and transformed his life (1 Timothy 1:12-14). He was grateful for his salvation and would not boast in anything except the cross of the Lord Jesus (Galatians 6:14). Paul wanted people to be impressed with Christ, not him.

> Paul wanted people to be impressed with Christ, not him.

Paul also exemplified the paradoxes of Christianity, specifically the closer we grow to God—the more sinful we may actually feel. If that sounds puzzling, the next chapter entitled "The Paradox of Holiness" will further explain this conundrum. Paul experienced first-hand another paradox as revealed in 2 Corinthians 12:7-10. When we are weak, it is then that we are strong. When we realize our weakness, we go to Christ for strength and rely on him. When we feel strong and self-confident, we neglect Christ and rely on ourselves. Paul also taught biblically balanced Christianity and lived with the tension that he was a new creation still living in the old creation.

The classic book *Life Together* by Dietrich Bonhoeffer contains a section on the ministry of meekness. Bonhoeffer insists we must perceive ourselves as the greatest of sinners. This is difficult for us to admit, because it:

> arouses all the resistance of the natural man, but also that of the self-confident Christian. It sounds like an exaggeration, like an untruth. Yet even Paul said of himself that he was the foremost of sinners… there can be no genuine acknowledgement of sin that does not lead to this extremity.[44]

Bonhoeffer goes on to explain that if we are viewing our personal sin as smaller and less serious in comparison to other people, we are failing to truly grasp our own sinful condition. If we look at another person and consider their sin worse than ours, we lack humility and are putting ourselves above them.

John declares that "if we claim to be without sin, we deceive ourselves and the truth is not in us" (1 John 1:8). The mere fact that we are instructed to confess our sins to God (1 John 1:9) and to each other (James 5:16) should clarify that Christians still sin. As Brennan Manning words it in *The Ragamuffin Gospel*, we all wear "tilted halos."

The New Testament contains multiple letters that Paul wrote to Christian believers. Paul frequently addressed the believers as saints. The word saint, by the way, simply refers to being "set apart" or to being a "holy one." However, we should be struck by the ironic fact that after Paul addressed these people as saints, his letters often go on to speak of their struggles with sinful behavior. R.C. Sproul states that "The saints of Scripture were called saints not because they were already pure but because they were people who were set apart and called to purity."[45] They were still works in progress, as Paul also asserted about himself in Philippians 3:12-14. He had not arrived at his goal, but he would press forward in order to take hold of that for which Christ Jesus took hold of him.

Simul Justus et Peccator

To answer the question of whether we are saints or sinners, Martin Luther coined the now famous Latin phrase: *"Simul Justus et Peccator."* It means that Christians are simultaneously saints and sinners: *Simul* (at the same time), *Justus* (just or righteous), *Peccator* (a sinner). We have been justified—declared righteous in the sight of God based on Christ's work for us—even though we still commit sin in this life. We are redeemed sinners, and admitting our sin does not mean we are overlooking who we are in Christ. Chapter 8 will elaborate on the great doctrine of justification and the Christian's secure position in Christ.

I prefer to think of myself as a "saint and sinner" but viewing yourself as "a saint who sins" is also an option. Some may prefer how the slightly different wording of the later stresses our identity and position in Christ while still acknowledging our sin. The danger lies in seeing yourself as *only* a saint. Jerry Bridges states:

> If we refuse to identify ourselves as sinners as well as saints, we risk the danger of deceiving ourselves about our sin and becoming like the self-righteous Pharisee. Our hearts are deceitful (Jeremiah 17:9), and we all have moral 'blind spots.' We have a difficult enough time seeing our sin without someone insisting that we no longer consider ourselves as 'sinners.' [46]

Nevertheless, some people insist it is important, even critical, to focus primarily or only on our saintly status—believing that we become what we think we are. This reasoning asserts that if we think of ourselves as sinners, we will be more likely to act like sinners. Likewise, if we think of ourselves as saints, we will be more inclined to act like saints. There are multiple concerns with this perspective. As Bridges pointed out, as well as previous portions of this book, we have a natural tendency towards pride and self-delusion. Focusing only on our saintly status will feed this weakness, as well as set us up for a fall into sin by lowering our level of awareness.

We Become What We Think We Are?

Of equal concern is the underlying belief that "we become what we think we are." Is this accurate? It does not appear to be a biblical teaching. Scripture does urge us to think about worthy things, and what we think about can affect our behavior for good or for bad. However, the concept of becoming what we think we are is another thing entirely. It bears the marks of the positive thinking and self-affirmation approach, but more than that, it is grounded in distinctly New Thought and Eastern religious principles. Remember that the basic premises of New Thought were human-centered, and thoughts were elevated to mystical heights.

A short book published in 1902 by James Allen entitled *As a Man Thinketh* rose in popularity and brought New Thought ideas to more people. Interestingly, the book is still in print today. Its popularity in the early twentieth century led to the phrase "as a man thinketh" becoming the informal motto of the New Thought movement. James Allen was heavily influenced by Buddhism, transcendentalism, and other Eastern religious concepts. Ironically, he took his title from Proverbs 23:7 in the Bible. However, the verse is taken entirely out of context. Even Christians today take the isolated phrase "as a man thinketh" (that's the King James) and use it to promote the power of our thoughts.

Read in context, Proverbs 23:6-7 has nothing to do with the power of our thoughts. On the contrary, it is a warning against deceptive motives of the heart. An individual may do something generous, yet be inwardly stingy, and possess ulterior motives for their generosity. Mitch Horowitz makes the observation that this type of misuse of sources was common in New Thought and the early positive thinking movement. They wanted their ideas to be understood as matching or completing ancient beliefs. He states that "they tended to retrofit the positivity gospel to Scripture and other antique sources, sometimes ignoring the context of favored passages."[47] It continues to happen today.

Rhonda Byrne, author of *The Secret* mentioned in chapter 1, utterly misuses Matthew 21:22 and even claims that the method she teaches is based on the New Testament.[48] Her teachings could not be more distant from orthodox Christianity! Sadly, even Christian authors do a similar thing when they distort Scripture to make ideas about positive thinking or prosperity match the Bible. It is startling to observe actual endorsement of New Thought writers. In one of her recent best-selling books, a Christian author references James Allen to support ideas about the power of our thoughts. A large online Christian book retailer has several editions of *As a Man Thinketh* for sale. While there is truth to be found outside of the Bible, our beliefs particularly about the spiritual life should flow from the Word of God and a distinctly biblical worldview.

Every religion agrees that the world is not the way it should be, and each religion prescribes a solution to what is considered the problem. New Thought was shaped partly by Eastern religious ideas, and most religions of the Far East teach that the basic human problem is intellectual or involves ignorance, with various paths to reach enlightenment or liberation.[49] Christianity teaches that the basic human problem is moral; we are helpless sinners in need of a Savior. As stated in chapter 3, if you mess up the problem (sin) you mess up the solution (Christ and his great salvation). It should be evident that theories stemming from Eastern religious principles will offer flawed solutions.

Our thoughts about ourselves should not be viewed as the key for successful Christian living. There is danger in locating our hope in anything *inside* of us. John Stott refers to an archbishop who defined original sin as being "twisted with self-centeredness."[50] Anything that encourages this self-ward tendency cannot be beneficial. Instead, our hope should be *external* in the promises of God in Jesus. In 2 Corinthians 4:5-7 Paul emphasizes that believers are not

> Our hope should be *external* in the promises of God in Jesus.

proclaiming themselves but Jesus, and power comes from God—not from us. Oswald Chambers, in a devotional from *My Utmost for His Highest*, states:

> What shines forth and reveals God in your life is not your relative consistency to an idea of what a saint should be, but your genuine, living relationship with Jesus Christ, and your unrestrained devotion to him.[51]

Where is your unrestrained devotion? Is it Christ, or your saintliness? We can inadvertently make an idol out of our spiritual life, our holiness, or our progress in the faith—similar to how New Thought and positive thinking make an idol of our success in this life.

Conflict from Within and Without

Part of the problem may be that we are looking for shortcuts to make things easier or speed us along in our faith journey. Relying on positive thoughts surely seems a useful option for becoming successful in our Christian life. More realistically, I once heard our Christian life described as a "long obedience in the same direction."[52] Reading through the New Testament over several months, I noticed a repeated emphasis on finishing the Christian life and enduring to the end. We are told to press forward, run the race, persevere, be patient, put forth effort, and maintain an eternal perspective. Life in the present time is not one of ease; we are to be watching, praying, fighting, working, obeying, and keeping the faith. Jesus tells a brief story in Mark 13:33-37 to remind his followers to be working while the master is away and be alert and on guard for his return.

Hebrews 12:1-2 compares the Christian life to a race that requires perseverance. It is not a leisurely stroll, nor is it a fifty-yard dash. It is more like a marathon. We are exhorted to "throw off everything that hinders and the sin that so easily entangles" us. Even a Christian running the race of faith can get easily—note easily—ensnared by sin. We are not above its enticement. We are also instructed in verse 2 to fix our eyes on Jesus, who is the finish line of the race. A runner in a race cannot get distracted. It is easy to fix our eyes on our goals, our purpose, our victory. This certainly does not mean we should be aimless in our Christian life, but where is our ultimate focus? If we are absorbed with ourselves, we are running in circles and towards a nonexistent finish line. We will soon become exhausted and our efforts futile. May each of us proclaim with Paul: "my only aim is to finish the race and complete the task the Lord Jesus has given me—the task of testifying to the good news of God's grace" (Acts 20:24).

Some theologies give the impression that those who struggle in the Christian life are subpar Christians. The classic allegorical work *Pilgrim's Progress* by John Bunyan has fallen on hard times among some Christians today. The path to the Celestial City was filled with challenges: fights, fears, and temptations from within and without. Certain Christians don't appreciate this emphasis, and feel an optimistic expectation is better. But is that the reality?

It is true that one passage on this issue (Romans 7) can be interpreted in different ways, but I happen to think it does refer to a Christian. We may be new creations in Christ, but vestiges of our old self remain and the potential to sin is there. Galatians chapter 5 contains similar content, particularly verse 17 which highlights the conflict between the flesh and spirit and the struggle to do the right thing. This is not insinuating that Christians should be struggling all the time. We can overcome certain sin in our life, and the Holy Spirit can transform some aspects of our being. Yet rather than downplay the conflict between the flesh and spirit, the apostle Paul states it plainly and openly. It is evidence that we are living in the already but not yet. We have divided hearts that will not be whole until eternity.

Have we forgotten about Ephesians 6? It contains the well-known "armor of God" passage. If we are not involved in a cosmic struggle, why would we be instructed to put on all these pieces of armor? Believers are clearly in a supernatural battle as they live in this world. Verse 12 reminds us that "our struggle is not against flesh and blood, but against… the spiritual forces of evil in the heavenly realms." We need to be prepared and to remember that we have a very real enemy: Satan and his demonic gang.

> Conflict is inevitable when you are living in a way that directly opposes the world.

Paul instructed Timothy to "fight the good fight of the faith" and to join him in suffering "like a good soldier of Christ Jesus" (1 Timothy 6:12; 2 Timothy 2:3). Conflict is inevitable when you are living in a way that directly opposes the world. Even Jesus was not exempt from temptation from the devil, and in Luke 4 we can read about his temptation in the wilderness. Observe that Luke 4:1 says that Jesus was "full of the Holy Spirit" and "led by the Spirit" at this time. Being in a good spiritual state does not make us immune to temptation. In fact, that may precisely be when Satan decides to tempt us. J.C. Ryle summarizes:

> We may take comfort about our souls if we know anything of an inward fight and conflict. It is the invariable companion of genuine Christian holiness. It is not everything, I am well aware, but it is something. Do we find in our heart of hearts a spiritual struggle? Do we feel anything of the flesh lusting against the spirit and the spirit against the flesh, so that we cannot do the things we would? (Gal. 5:17)…Well, let us thank God for it! It is a good sign. It is strongly probable evidence of the great work of sanctification…Anything is better than apathy, stagnation, deadness, and indifference.[53]

If a person is finding the Christian life primarily one of ease, it should be a warning sign that something is wrong. Are you truly living as a Christian in this world? If you have little or no sin that you struggle with, this suggests some introspection is in order. Has the secular culture desensitized you to the point where you are indifferent to sin? Perhaps, like the church of Laodicea in Revelation 3, you are self-deceived and need Jesus to reveal the truth about yourself. There is always hope.

Laodicea was reminded that Jesus rebukes those he loves, and Jesus told them to be earnest and repent. Furthermore, Jesus beckons them in verse 20: "Here I am! I stand at the door and knock. If anyone hears my voice and opens the door, I will come in and eat with that person, and they with me." They could be in fellowship with Jesus once again, as can each of us if we have wandered away from our Savior. As will be covered in the next chapter, often the way up is actually down. Humbly admitting our sin can open the door to more abundant life.

Questions for Reflection and Discussion

1. What are the dangers of overemphasizing either our saintliness or our sinfulness? Worded another way, what are the benefits of maintaining a saint and sinner tension?
2. We are to be moving forward in our faith, and Hebrews 12:1 says we should throw off everything that hinders us. What things are hindering you? How can you throw them off?
3. Do you empathize with the inner struggle to do right?
4. What we think about is important, but how is that different from ascribing special power to our thoughts? Look up Romans 1:16; 2 Peter 1:2-3; 1 Corinthians 1:18, 24; 2 Corinthians 4:7. Where is the Christian's source of power?

Chapter 6

The Paradox of Holiness

There are only two kinds of men: the righteous, who
believe themselves sinners; the rest, sinners who believe
themselves righteous. —Blaise Pascal

God creates out of nothing. Therefore, until a man is nothing,
God can make nothing out of him. —Martin Luther

Some Christians grow; others just swell.
—Attributed to an old preacher

As you mature in your faith should you begin to feel more holy
or spiritually successful? Should the growing saint feel saintly? I
was once told by a Christian that he perceived his good deeds as
a pleasing aroma to God. I suppose this is true in a certain sense
because God is pleased when we are obedient and we may sense
God's pleasure as we serve him. Psalm 147:11 says that "the Lord
delights in those who fear him, who put their hope in his unfailing
love." But we want to become holier, not holier-than-thou. If our
daily perception of our self is that we are a spiritual success whose
deeds delight God, it should be a warning that things are not as

well with us spiritually as we think. It is illogical to elevate ourselves yet assume we are growing closer to the image of our Savior who humbled himself.

Consider humility. It's a paradox: truly humble people do not realize they are humble. The moment you think you are humble, you have, in fact, lost your humility! Isaiah 57:15 states:

> For this is what the high and exalted One says—he who lives forever, whose name is holy: 'I live in a high and holy place, but also with the one who is contrite and lowly in spirit, to revive the spirit of the lowly and to revive the heart of the contrite.'

It almost seems like a contradiction: God dwells in a high and holy place, but he also dwells with the contrite and lowly. It is a startling contrast: we get close to God by realizing how far we are from him. It is when we gaze upon God and realize how desperately we fall short of his glory and perfection that God comes near and revives our hearts. Jesus taught similar principles in the renowned Beatitudes in his Sermon on the Mount (Matthew 5). The "blessed" are those who are poor in spirit, mournful, and meek—those who realize they come to the spiritual table with nothing to offer. Is this how we typically perceive blessing? I dare say not.

Isaiah 6 contains Isaiah's famous vision of God in the temple. The scene is one of glorious majesty. God is high and exalted, and the seraphim cry out, "Holy, holy, holy is the Lord Almighty; the whole earth is full of his glory" (verse 3). Isaiah is intensely humbled, and his response in verse 5 was: "Woe to me!...I am ruined! For I am a man of unclean lips, and I live among a people of unclean lips, and my eyes have seen the King, the Lord Almighty." As God's prophet, Isaiah was essentially God's "lips" declaring God's Words to the people, yet he declares his lips unclean. The closer one gets to a physical light, the brighter it shines and the more it reveals. Likewise, when seeing himself next to God's majestic holiness, Isaiah's own sinfulness was all the more evident to himself.

Have You Been Ruined?

Several years ago I came across a contemporary Christian song based on Isaiah's experience entitled "Ruin Me." Even though it was deeply moving, I've never again heard it on the radio or in a church setting. Sadly, I'm not surprised. In a culture of positive thinking and self-affirmation, singing about being "ruined" by an encounter with God is not very appealing. Yet after Isaiah said "woe is me" the seraphim in the vision touched his lips with coal from the altar and proclaimed that his sin was forgiven. Then, for the first time in the vision, God spoke to Isaiah.

Humility makes room for a transforming encounter with God. For such a contrite heart, there was immediate mercy. Confession and humility bring us closer to the

> Humility makes room for a transforming encounter with God.

Lord. Self-righteousness and arrogance keep God at a distance. In the Beatitudes, it is the "blessed" who *see God* and find comfort. When we realize our humble place before the mighty and majestic God, we have opened the door for the Lord to minister to us. This is a place of hope and revival, not despair and despondency! F.B. Meyer makes this touching and astute observation:

> I used to think that God's gifts were on shelves one above the other; and that the taller we grew in Christian character the easier we could reach them. I now find that God's gifts are on shelves one beneath the other; and it is not a question of growing

> taller but of stooping lower; and that we have to go
> down, always down, to get His best gifts.[54]

Is this experience unique to Isaiah? Definitely not; there are similar examples elsewhere in the Scripture. Encounters with God humbled people, and they fell down or otherwise bemoaned their sinfulness. Job was a righteous man who endured terrible trials. Towards the end of his suffering, *after* Job had encountered God, his response was: "I am unworthy—how can I reply to you? I put my hand over my mouth....Therefore I despise myself and repent in dust and ashes" (Job 40:4; 42:6). God never answered Job's questions, but revealed himself to Job in all his majesty. Randy Alcorn says that whenever he needs an attitude adjustment, he reads the last five chapters of Job.

> God's powerful self-revelation to this man who
> endured such suffering offers great perspective. At
> the end of the book the focus shifts from Job's
> suffering to God's majesty. I never read those
> chapters without feeling that God has been put in
> his proper place and I've been put in mine.[55]

Job responded to God's self-revelation with silence and repentance. Not until Job reached this point did he find comfort. He had encountered God, and that was sufficient.

New Testament examples abound. Seeing Christ perform a miracle in Luke 5, Peter "fell at Jesus' knees and said, 'Go away from me, Lord; I am a sinful man!'" (verse 8). Something about the miracle must have overpowered Peter with a sense of the disparity between him and Jesus. It appears that when there is a display of divine glory, there is a corresponding sense of human guilt.

The apostle John responds in kind when he had his grand vision of the exalted Christ on Patmos. He fell at Christ's feet as though dead (Revelation 1:17). Even though John was an intimate companion of Jesus, in this encounter John is over-awed at his majesty. After John lay prostrate, Jesus placed his hand on John and told him not to be afraid; what a gracious and reassuring response by our Lord. The humble man was brought close. John was then given the task of recording the message that would be revealed to him.

In a similar way, it was after being humbled by the majestic vision of God in the temple that Isaiah responded "Here am I. Send me!" (Isaiah 6:8) to God's inquiry about who would do his bidding. The apostle Paul reminds us in 2 Corinthians 12:9-10 that it is not our weakness that will get in the way of God working through us, but our delusion of strength. When John and Isaiah were humbled, it gave way to obedience, and they were ready to be utilized by God.

God's Unlikely Talent Pool

The world tends to value power, capability, and charisma but God's ways are different. As humility can prepare us for service, God also seeks out those for his purposes who do not meet the expected qualifications. In unfortunate contrast, many Christian motivational books and sermons encourage us to affirm ourselves, concentrating on our abilities and the ways God can use us. Imagine if Moses or Jeremiah or Gideon had read some of these books or heard some of these sermons. When God approached them, they likely would have enthusiastically replied that they were ready and given God a verbal resume of their talents. The actual replies of these men were not necessarily ideal and ensued from deficient faith or fear. They offered excuses: decrying their youth, poor communication skills, and lack of family status. What they didn't realize was that they had exactly the lack of qualifications God was looking for! God has a consistent habit of using the unlikely and the unimportant (1 Corinthians 1:26-31), and even those full of excuses.

A little self-doubt can be a good thing, and total confidence can actually be an indicator that you are not ready for the task. God wants people who are depending upon him, not on themselves. G.K. Chesterton, writing in 1908, critiques the idea of "believing in yourself" as the key to success. He refers to "ugly individualistic philosophy" and says you are more likely to fail when you have total self-confidence. In Chesterton's unique straightforward way, he states: "Complete self-confidence is not merely sin; complete self-confidence is a weakness. Believing utterly in one's self is a hysterical and superstitious belief."[56] The question then arises: if we are not to believe in our self, what then are we to believe in? Chesterton says he wrote his book *Orthodoxy,* an apologetic defense of Christianity, to answer that very question. As the door of self-confidence slams shut, the windows of our heart can open to the wonders of God's grace through Christ.

In Acts 4, Peter and John respond to the objections of some religious leaders. When these leaders "saw the courage of Peter and John and realized that they were *unschooled, ordinary men*, they were astonished and they took note that these men *had been with Jesus*" (verse 13, emphasis added). God can certainly use educated and exceptional people too, but insufficiency is an advantage in Christianity as it demonstrates that our sufficiency is from God. There is also a risk that our abilities can overshadow Jesus Christ instead of pointing people to Christ. Indeed, an influential and gifted American pastor stepped down from his ministry several years ago precisely because he felt that *his* persona was eclipsing Jesus Christ. He continues to be used by God in other less overt and behind the scene ways.

We All Fall Short

As initially emphasized, an encounter with God increases our sense of his holiness and our own unworthiness. This applies to everyone. We often speak of reprobates needing to have the "fear of God" put into them. It would fit our frame of reference for God to pull an unrepentant thug out of prison and give him a grand vision of himself in order to induce a mournful repentance. It seems right that a criminal needs to be humbled in this way before God. However, observe that Isaiah, Job, Peter, and John were essentially "good" men when they were cut to the core by their encounters with God. Job, in particular, was declared to be a blameless and upright man who feared God and shunned evil (Job 1:8). John, on Patmos, had already been a faithful servant of Jesus for many years. Even "good guys" and mature believers fall short of God's glory (Romans 3:23).

Acknowledging your sin does not mean you are a failure in the spiritual life. In fact, there seems a clear paradox of holiness. The holier and less sinful we become, the more unholy and sinful we may actually feel. Are you confused? As we mature in our faith, our spiritual vision becomes clearer. Past sins previously overlooked may become apparent to us for the first time. As we grow in the likeness of Jesus, we become more sensitive to sins that still remain in our life. The more precious our Savior becomes to us, the more we should want to please him. While the following excerpt is a bit lengthy, I think it is a real gem from A.W. Tozer:

> The purest souls never knew how pure they were
> and the greatest saints never guessed that they were
> great. The very thought that they were good or great
> would have been rejected by them as a temptation of
> the devil. They were so engrossed with gazing upon
> the face of God that they spent scarce a moment
> looking at themselves. They were suspended in that
> sweet paradox of spiritual awareness where they
> knew that they were clean through the blood of
> the Lamb and yet felt that they deserved only death

and hell as their reward. This feeling is strong in
the writings of Paul and is found in almost all the
devotional books and among the greatest and most
loved hymns.[57]

Surely it is a sweet paradox of spiritual awareness. Tozer was
writing in the 1950's and I'm not so sure that his entire last sentence
holds true today. Many of our modern devotionals and songs are
painfully anemic spiritually, biblically, and doctrinally. I think this
is primarily because we have lost sight of the majesty of God.

Rediscovering the Majesty of God

In modern Christianity, particularly in evangelical circles, we
have stressed that God is personal and that we can have a personal
relationship with him through Christ. This is true, and in a certain
way it cannot be overemphasized. The God who came near through
the Incarnation of Jesus is the unique truth of Christianity that
must be proclaimed. We do not serve a deistic God who created
humanity and disappeared, but a personal God who cared so much
about his creation that he entered into it. God became one of us
and opened the way for us to be in a relationship with God through
Jesus the Son.

However, we cannot forget that God is still God. We
have emphasized God's immanence at the expense of God's
transcendence. As Leslie Leyland Fields states:

> As evangelicals, we believe that God can be
> known intimately, so we urge believers towards a
> 'personal relationship with Jesus.' But from what
> I've witnessed, it can become so personal it ends up
> being about the wrong person—me. [58]

We reduced the distance between creature and Creator and lost a reverence or healthy fear for God. Far too many contemporary Christian books, sermons, and songs have an individualistic focus—it is all about me and Jesus. God is for us (Romans 8:31), but not in the egotistical manner that has become commonplace. In forgetting God's majesty much is lost. When we lose sight of God's greatness, we lose the very reason that makes his personal nature so significant and meaningful.

In an article about the need to re-discover God's holiness, Drew Dyck writes:

> The cruel irony of choosing God's love over his holiness is that we end up losing both. The affection of a familiar, buddy deity isn't worth much. Only the Lord of heaven and earth, who dwells in unapproachable light, is truly awe-inspiring. When we lose sight of God's greatness, his love loses meaning.[59]

We have all encountered different types of leaders and bosses in our life. Some bosses lead from the distance and are rarely involved with the day-to-day functions of the business performed by the employees. My husband and I share the same profession, and our managers often have that style. But we have also had managers with a more personal manner who would sometimes join us and offer assistance in a time of need. This was an incredible morale booster. It is one thing for a co-worker to help another co-worker, but for the boss to do so speaks volumes. The best functioning department I ever experienced in my work history was led by a manager with both an authoritative *and* personal style. You may have also encountered a boss who was personal but lacked authority, and this caused a myriad of problems. It is difficult to exercise authority when you are trying to be everyone's friend. Can you picture these illustrations in relation to God?

We do not want a God who is *only* our friend. What kind of God would that be? We have domesticated God to our peril and created a false god of our own making. Yet we don't want a distant or strictly authoritarian deity either. Thankfully, through Christ, we have both. Hebrews 4:15-16 gives us the reassuring reminder that we have a God who can sympathize with us because he knows what it is like to be human. As we celebrate at Christmas time, the little baby in the manger is also the omnipotent Creator of the heavens and earth. It is God's majesty and transcendence that makes his personal outreach to humanity so awe-inspiring! We need a renewed vision of God's greatness. It will infuse our spiritual lives with depth and rescue us from a superficial, individualistic, and self-centered faith.

> We need a renewed vision of God's greatness.

Holiness: What's That?

The words holy and holiness may be uncertain or unfamiliar to you depending on your church background. The apostle Peter said in 1 Peter 1:15 that "just as he who called you is holy, so be holy in all you do" and he goes on to quote the Old Testament. A Christian should be holy or progressing in holiness. In a general sense, this is simply referring to how we should be growing in the Christian life. Maybe instead of holiness, you are more familiar with terms like discipleship, sanctification, godliness, Christian maturity, or spiritual transformation. These are different words with varying nuances of meaning, but each are speaking of the same broad idea of our becoming more like Jesus and experiencing the fruit of the

Spirit in our life. However, let's step back and consider the word holy in relation to God.

Our word holy is translated from the ancient Hebrew language where it is associated with the ideas of purity and righteousness. In addition, the concept of holiness carried the idea of being separate, set part, or transcendent. The word could describe something or someone—people, a nation, or objects—that is set apart from the common for God's service. R.C. Sproul in his classic book *The Holiness of God* points out that when we typically use the word holy to describe God, we use it as one word among many in a list of God's attributes: God is loving, holy, just, omnipotent, merciful, etc. Sproul adds:

> But when the word holy is applied to God, it does not signify one single attribute. On the contrary, God is called holy in a general sense. The word is used as a synonym for his deity. That is, the word holy calls attention to all that God is.[60]

Everything about God is holy, and all his attributes could have the word holy placed before them—holy love, holy justice, holy mercy, and so on. The word transcendent is also critical. Everything about God is above and beyond us. God is separate and distinct from the world he created, and while we as Christians are called to be holy we cannot be holy in the same sense that God is holy. Our love for others will never match up to God's holy love, yet as Christians we are called to live differently in this world and reflect our Creator.

God's holiness is the *only* aspect of God that is elevated to the third degree, that is, mentioned three times in succession. As we looked at in Isaiah 6:3, the seraphim cry out, "Holy, holy, holy is the Lord Almighty; the whole earth is full of his glory." In the New Testament, in Revelation 4:8, we can similarly observe the living creatures around God's throne crying out non-stop: "Holy, holy, holy is the Lord God Almighty, who was, and is, and is to come." In regards to Isaiah 6:3, Sproul shares that this repetition of a word is a device used in ancient Hebrew to emphasize a point. In modern English, we would typically *italicize*, **bold**, or use an exclamation point to show importance. Observe that it is not love, love, love or mercy, mercy, mercy. Yes, God is loving and merciful but it is only God's holiness that receives this special emphasis. We should pay attention! Luke 1 contains Mary's Magnificat, her song. In verse 49 she proclaims "the Mighty One has done great things for me—holy is his name." Even God's name is holy, and that is because he is holy.

When leading a Bible study on the opening chapters of Revelation, a revealing activity can be having everyone share one-word or brief phrase descriptions of Jesus. Then have the group read Revelation 1:9-20 and share the words that come to their mind after contemplating this passage. It portrays the grand and exalted Jesus in all his glory. A very different set of words will likely be the result. It is not that one set of words is right and the other wrong, but it illuminates our one-sided view of Jesus. The positive thinking paradigm infiltrated our churches and distracted us from God's holiness by shifting the focus to ourselves. J.I. Packer in his classic work *Knowing God*, states that:

> The Christian's instincts of trust and worship are stimulated very powerfully by knowledge of the greatness of God. But this is knowledge which Christians today largely lack; and that is one reason why our faith is so feeble and our worship so flabby. We are modern people, and modern people, though they cherish great thoughts of themselves, have as a rule small thoughts of God.[61]

When we elevate ourselves, we lose sight of God's greatness. It is not that humanity lacks value, worth, and dignity because we do have these things in the eyes of God—but the teeter-totter slammed down in the direction of self. Humanity became the beginning point instead of God. First Peter 1:16 states that we are to be holy because God is holy. First John 4:7-21 emphasizes the love of God, and states that we are to love because God first loved us. The word *because* is critical and should not be overlooked. God is the fountainhead of our lives. For the majority of us, our thoughts of God are not great enough. We need to be "ruined" by an encounter with the majestic and holy God, and then we will be astonished by the door that was opened by Jesus for bold and personal access to the God of the universe (Hebrews 4:16). What a privilege and honor to enter through it.

Questions for Reflection and Discussion

1. It is one thing to acknowledge we are sinful; it is another to actually grieve or mourn over it. Have you had a "woe is me" experience?
2. Do you think there is enough sorrow for personal sin among Christians? Consider reading Psalm 51. Second Corinthians 7:8-10 says Godly sorrow should lead to what?
3. What could be some warning signs that you have domesticated or sentimentalized God in your life?
4. Hebrews 12:28 says we should "worship God acceptably with reverence and awe." How can you better worship God with reverence and awe?

Chapter 7

A Christian View of Self

Boasting is evidence that we are pleased with self; belittling,
that we are disappointed in it. Either way, we reveal that
we have a high opinion of ourselves. —A.W. Tozer

Not to us, Lord, not to us but to your name be the glory,
because of your love and faithfulness. —Psalm 115:1

Knowing God without knowing our own wretchedness makes
for pride. Knowing our own wretchedness without knowing God
makes for despair. Knowing Jesus Christ strikes the balance,
because he shows us both God and our own wretchedness.
—Blaise Pascal

It is a common assumption in our society that in order to live a
productive and happy life, an individual must possess high self-
esteem or have a good self-image. This modern-day concept is an
anomaly and lacks logical underpinnings. While humility has not
been equally valued in all times and places, it has generally been
considered a commendable virtue. In contrast, as the twentieth
century progressed, it reached a point where blatant self-regard was

no longer viewed with alarm and a modest view of self was even perceived as a weakness.

Timothy Keller points out that up until the twentieth century, traditional cultures believed that it was pride or too high a view of self that was the root cause of evil in the world.[62] The consensus took a dramatic turn in the twentieth century, particularly in the western world. Low self-esteem came to be viewed as the root cause of problems.

There is a distinct connection with New Thought and the power of positive thinking that took the twentieth century by storm. Thinking positively about yourself and your future became the core philosophy in life. It should not be a surprise that this led to a widespread preoccupation with self, as we observed the development of the self-esteem movement in the 1970's and 1980's. Secular psychology and social-science during those years promoted the importance of self-esteem, emphasizing that increased self-esteem would solve many social ills. High self-esteem was going to improve academic performance in schools and decrease crime and drug abuse in society.

The emphasis on self-esteem moved into the church during those years. Robert Schuller, the American pastor and motivational speaker of Crystal Cathedral fame, promoted self-esteem and "possibility thinking" in Christian circles. Schuller even wrote a book with the revealing title of *Self Esteem: The New Reformation*.

> It is not God's purpose to glorify us, but for us to glorify him.

His premise was that similar to how the sixteenth century Reformation led to a paradigm shift, we now needed a new reformation to focus on the sacred right of every person to self-esteem. Schuller suggests that, "What we need is a theology of salvation that begins and ends with recognition of every person's hunger for glory."[63] The theological problems with this statement should be evident. Our hunger for glory? What about

God's glory? It is not God's purpose to glorify us, but for us to glorify him. Schuller was a protégé of Norman Vincent Peale. Peale's beliefs, while cushioned in Christian language, were grounded in New Thought ideology as discussed in chapter one. We can observe the continued trickle down influence of New Thought.

Psychologist Lauren Slater wrote an article in 2002 for *The New York Times* magazine entitled "The Trouble with Self-Esteem" in which she critiques the self-esteem methodology.[64] While self-esteem was touted as the cure to all social problems, in all actuality, it did not work. The promised results of an improved society did not materialize. Slater references several studies which revealed it was high self-esteem—rather than low—which created problems and posed a greater threat to society. *Oops!* As Christians with a biblical worldview, we should have known this all along. We did not need secular research to tell us this, although the confirmation is helpful and reassuring. The self-esteem approach played right into the inherent human weakness, emphasized throughout the Bible, that humanity has core issues with pride. Also fascinating is that Slater traces the beginnings of the self-esteem movement all the way back to "mind cure" (or mental healing) in the late nineteenth century. Mental healing was the forerunner to New Thought. This mindset is hard to break, and Slater observes that:

> Self-esteem, as a construct, as a quasi religion, is woven into a tradition that both defines and confines us as Americans. If we were to deconstruct self-esteem, to question its value, we would be, in a sense, questioning who we are, nationally and individually. We would be threatening our self-esteem.[65]

It is almost like secular blasphemy to criticize self-esteem and instead emphasize a humble and cautious view of the self, but the tide is beginning to turn slowly in our society. I was amused by a recent insurance commercial that showed Pinocchio teaching a motivational class. As Pinocchio enthusiastically shouted about the positive potential of the audience, his nose began to grow longer and longer. The self-affirmation mindset must continue to be deconstructed, and it may take another generation to even begin to chip away at the wall of positive thinking that was erected during the twentieth century.

Avoiding False Dichotomies

What should be a Christian view of self? Part of the problem is that we can only seem to think in polar opposites, creating false dichotomies. If we do not think positively, that means we have to think negatively. If we do not have a positive view of ourselves, that means we must hate ourselves. These are not the only options! Optimism or pessimism often keeps us absorbed with ourselves, either on our capabilities or failures. Instead I advocate for biblical realism grounded in our identity in Christ.

Timothy Keller has observed that the gospel humbles us to the dust but also exalts us to the heavens. Or as previously referenced by Mark McMinn, we are noble ruins: both noble and ruined at the same time. Psalm 8:4-6 gives such dignity to humanity:

> What is mankind that you are mindful of them, human beings that you care for them? You have made them a little lower than the angels and crowned them with glory and honor. You made them rulers over the works of your hands; you put everything under their feet.

Human beings are made in the image of their Creator and are noble creations given the privilege of ruling in this world (Genesis 1:26). The theological term for this is the *Imago Dei*, which applies exclusively to humans. We have a unique imprint placed upon us by God, and we reflect God in a way that other creatures do not. This Judeo-Christian teaching gives intrinsic value to all humans, and has led to Christians worldwide being involved in countless acts of service helping the sick, orphaned, destitute, imperiled, addicted, homeless, or otherwise down and out.[66] Even in the individual whose life has been terribly marred by sin or suffering, we can see vestiges of the image of God if we only have eyes to see it. We can fail in this area, and some of us need to improve at seeing the image of God in everyone. Look for the good in each person; it is there.

At the same time, observe the emphasis in Psalm eight. The first and last verses (1 and 9) are identical and state: "Lord, our Lord, how majestic is your name in all the earth!" Humanity is elevated, but it is cushioned between statements about God's greatness. Our worth flows from who God is as the Creator. God is paramount. Conversely, the self-esteem or positive thinking perspective puts a narcissistic spin on it. God is neglected, and the emphasis is on the worthiness of humanity. This can spill over into many things. An entitlement mentality can prevail, with an expectation that God owes us success or health or a trouble-free existence in this world.

An overemphasis on the worthiness of humanity can influence our approach to salvation. I think it is generally inadvertent, but it can come across that God sent his Son to redeem us *because of* our great worth. We want to be positive and encourage the individual: "You have great value to God." There is truth in that, as Jesus came to seek and save the lost (Luke 19:10). His very life demonstrated that Jesus cared for people, often reaching out to marginalized individuals in society. It's thought-provoking to note the different ways Jesus dealt with people. With those who realized they were sinners, Jesus brought dignity. With those who believed they were saints, Jesus brought chastening. While keeping these things in mind, we must not neglect a core teaching of Christianity about the sinfulness of humanity and the grace of God.

Bad News and Good News

God's grace is defined as the unmerited favor—the undeserved kindness—of God toward humanity. As a child, you may have learned a definition of grace based on each letter of the word: God's Riches at Christ's Expense. It is because of our sin that we need a Savior, and Jesus paid the price to bring us redemption. Romans 5:6-8 and Ephesians 2:1-5 emphasize that Christ died for us even though we were powerless, ungodly, sinful, deserving of wrath, and dead in transgressions. That is a dark portrait of humanity. God's love for us was not a response to our loveliness. The nature of grace is that it flows down from God to the ungodly.

> God's love for us was not a response to our loveliness.

Ephesians 2:4-5 states: "But because of his great love for us, God, who is rich in mercy, made us alive with Christ even when we were dead in transgressions—it is by grace you have been saved." Because? It is not because of our worthiness, but because of God's great love for us. We cannot transform ourselves; we are dead in sin. It is only through the power of Christ's life, death, and resurrection that we can be made alive with Christ. If we could transform ourselves, we would not need a Savior.

Even the Israelites in the Old Testament needed to be reminded of why God chose them as a special nation. In Deuteronomy 7:6-9, God said that is was not because they were a people great in number but because of God's love and his faithfulness to his covenant. Deuteronomy 9:4-6 further elaborates and triple emphasizes that it was not because of Israel's righteousness that he was bringing them to possess a land. It ends with an extra clear conclusion (verse 6): "Understand, then, that it is not because of your righteousness that the Lord your God is giving you this good land to possess, for you are a stiff-necked people." This blunt reminder would indicate that Israel had a problem with overestimating their integrity and were prone to forget their sinfulness. The problem rings through the ages and continues today.

It is precisely against this dark background of human sinfulness and pride that the gospel shines brightly and gives us hope. Amazing grace how sweet the sound that saved a wretch like me! When we lose sight of our wretchedness, God's grace is no longer amazing and actually loses its meaning of undeserved kindness. Did you know that the words of Amazing Grace are disturbing to some, so they alter the words? In modern times, the line "that saved a wretch like me" has been changed in some sources to "that saved and strengthened me" to avoid the condemnation of humanity. Singing about our wretchedness clashes with the pervasive societal obsession with self-affirmation.

A devotional I read spoke of the Romanticism that arose in the late eighteenth century as a reaction to the Age of Enlightenment. While there were some advantages to the exaltation of reason, something was lost. Romantic writers emphasized passion over reason, intuition over logic, and the majesty of nature over scientific analysis. The devotional quoted Marvin Olasky's description of the biblical worldview as "romantic realism":

> Christianity is both gruesomely accurate in its realistic depiction of abundant sin but also romantically hopeful— for the bridegroom, Christ, does not give up even when repeatedly spurned. The Bible is the romantic realist book that best shows both graves and grace. It doesn't pretend... but shows how we're all thigh deep in muck yet

able, through God's grace, to see the sun. Jesus not
only turned water into wine but turned Simon, who
dreamed of fish, into Peter, a fisher of men—and
he can do that to each of us.[67]

I appreciate the honest perspective of Christianity. We don't
have to pretend to be better than we are. You and I are not okay,
and that's okay, because there is ONE who bore our sin for us.
There is ONE who was perfect because we can't be, and that
perfect ONE gave his life for us (2 Corinthians 5:21). In spite of
our sins and failings, we are accepted because of what Jesus did
for us.

I heard about someone who began using the liturgy from a
high-church tradition in her personal devotional life, and the big
emphasis on humanity's sinfulness was at first a bit of a surprise.
Initially, she worried it would be discouraging or pessimistic (i.e.
damaging to the self-esteem), but she found that it actually had the
opposite effect. The honesty was refreshing. Sometimes she got
tired of fake, superficial, or obligatory praise from others. Or when
given an honest complement, she wondered what the person would
really think if they knew the darkest part of her heart. I think we
can all relate. The liturgy gave her hope because it pointed her to
Christ who gave his life for her despite her sinfulness. She was *thigh
deep in muck yet able, through God's grace, to see the sun.*

Self Esteem and the Christian

Self-esteem is typically understood as our feelings of worth
based on our capabilities, talents, or accomplishments in life. There
is indeed a proper, non-sinful "pride" where we can feel a sense of
satisfaction about a job well done. When God finished creating the
world in Genesis 1, God saw all that he made and it was proclaimed

to be very good. Certainly we can see our own accomplishments as very good. In *Mere Christianity,* C.S. Lewis makes a similar point that pleasure in being praised is not pride. The trouble begins when we move from being pleased by the acknowledgment, to thinking that we are great because of what we were praised about.[68]

The popular Christian motivational book that I refer to in chapter 2 proposes that we will find fulfillment in what we do for God, yet our fulfillment should ultimately come *from God* and not from what *we can do* for God. What if bad health or other changes in life prohibit us from doing the things that we were once doing for God? Where does that leave us? Our identity should be anchored in Christ and not in what we can do for Christ. Self-esteem that is primarily linked to what we can do can also lead us into prideful independence or arrogance about our capabilities.

Our abilities come from God, and we can easily end up elevating our gifts above the Giver of the gifts. The Bible teaches that God has given each of us spiritual gifts, and we should use the gifts we have *received* for God's glory (1 Peter 4:10-11). Those verses state in part that "If anyone serves, they should do so with the strength God provides, so that in all things God may be praised through Jesus Christ." We should serve in God's strength, not our strength. It is about God's glory, not our glory.

Jesus told a brief parable in Luke 17:7-10 that is applicable here. It mentions a farmhand who plows the fields and looks after the sheep for the owner. When the worker completes his tasks, does he then expect the boss to make him a meal and express gratitude to him for his work? No, the worker was just doing what he was hired to do. The parable concludes, "So you also, when you have done everything you were told to do, should say, 'We are unworthy servants; we have only done our duty.'" *Don't miss the point.* Jesus is trying to keep us from overestimating the value of our service or our own devotedness to him. In light of Calvary, we can hardly do too much or even enough for our Savior. At best, we are imperfect workers in his kingdom. We should not be expecting accolades, but should do our duty with gladness.

Have you considered that low self-esteem can be a form of pride? Two different people, one struggling with pride and the other with low self-esteem, can have the same core problem of self-absorption and self-centeredness. There is also "false humility" where some deprecate themselves for the sake of receiving praise from others. However, there are people who struggle with genuine low self-esteem. Regardless of the type of self-esteem struggle, is an ego message the answer? We can learn a great deal from God's response to Moses.

When God approached Moses in Exodus 3 and 4, Moses replied with the objection that he was a nobody ("who am I that I should go to Pharaoh?") and that he had inadequacies when it came to public speaking. Did God tell Moses that he should think more positively about himself and institute a self-affirmation regimen? *Uh, no.* In Exodus 3:12 and 4:11-12, God says to Moses:

> I will be with you....Who gave human beings their mouths? Who makes them deaf or mute? Who gives them sight or makes them blind? Is it not I, the Lord? Now go; I will help you speak and will teach you what to say.

Notice that God did not deny Moses's statement that he was a poor public speaker. We can have a tendency to offer false praise about someone's abilities in an effort to help them feel better about themselves or for our own ulterior motives. Moses was focused on himself, and God shifted the focus away from Moses to God. God encouraged Moses by emphasizing that he would be with Moses along the way. God would even tell Moses what to say so that he wouldn't be struggling with both his speaking ability and the content of his speeches.

This provides a helpful guide for us. An ego boosting message may actually exacerbate the problem. Instead, point the person to Christ and their identity or acceptance in him. Come along side of them, and be a support and encouragement. False affirmation and genuine encouragement are two different things. Be an encourager. Observe that God also told Moses to get moving ("now go") and do as God commanded him. Satisfaction or fulfillment is not found by pursuing it, but it comes as a *by-product* of obedience and faithful Christian living.

Thou Shalt Love Yourself?

What about Matthew 22:36-40? Doesn't the Bible tell us that we must love ourselves before we can love others well? This is a modern misinterpretation. Jesus was asked what the greatest commandment in the law was, and he answered that the first and greatest was "Love the Lord your God with all your heart and with all your soul and with all your mind." He continued: "And the second is like it: 'Love your neighbor as yourself.' All the Law and the Prophets hang on these two commandments."

Some people directly or indirectly turn this into three commandments: love God, love others, love yourself. Yet the passage itself emphasizes that it is two commandments, not three. Love God; love others. The verse presupposes that you already have a love for yourself. You clothe yourself, feed yourself, and look out for your own interests. This is natural. Jesus is telling his followers to go and do for others what they already do for themselves. Think of it in a Golden Rule type of way, as Matthew 7:12 states: "do to others what you would have them do to you." Furthermore, to see a command in Matthew 22:36-40 for an egotistic type of self-love contradicts the whole tenor of the New Testament and essence of Christianity.

Members of God's kingdom are told to deny themselves, and Jesus further says: "For whoever wants to save their life will lose it, but whoever loses their life for me will save it" (Luke 9: 23-24). The kingdom of God reverses our expectations! In John 12:24 Jesus, referring to his impending death, gives the illustration of a kernel of wheat. The kernel

> The kingdom of God reverses our expectations!

must fall to the ground and die, and it is only then that it produces many seeds. Likewise, through the death and resurrection of Jesus, salvation would be brought to humanity. This was a paradoxical way to save the world—the God of the universe relinquished his power, submitted to his enemies, and allowed himself to die.

Our natural tendency is to save our lives, but when we die to ourselves it gives way to new life in Jesus. I've heard it said that we should hide behind the cross. People should see Jesus through us, and we don't want to obstruct the view. The apostle Paul powerfully states in Galatians 2:20: "I have been crucified with Christ and I no longer live, but Christ lives in me. The life I now live in the body, I live by faith in the Son of God, who loved me and gave himself for me." We live on as individuals, but Christ now lives in us, and we are to live for him—not ourselves.

Also significant is 2 Timothy 3:1-5's list of sins that would be prevalent in the later days. Leading the list is that people would be *lovers of self*. The list concludes by stating that people would be lovers of pleasure rather than lovers of God. Rather than assuming that Christians would not drift into self-absorption, the New Testament warns us of the very real possibility (and reality) of it. We must continually look to Christ as our example.

Gospel Humility

As I come to the close of the chapter, I will attempt to summarize its content in case you are still unclear about how Christians should perceive themselves. I appreciated this statement from Thomas Tarrants, as he concludes his well-researched article on pride and humility:

> What is a right view of ourselves? Specifics will vary from person to person, but certain things are common to us all. We are God's creatures: small, finite, dependent, limited in intelligence and ability, prone to sin, and soon to die and face God's judgment (Heb. 9:27). But we are also God's children: created, loved, and redeemed by God's grace alone, not by anything in or of ourselves; and gifted by God with certain unique gifts, abilities, resources, and advantages, which are to be used for his glory. As Paul reminds the Corinthians, "What do you have that you did not receive? If then you received it, why do you boast as if you did not receive it?" (1 Cor. 4:7). Frequently reminding ourselves of these things is important.[69]

I also found some insights from Timothy Keller on "self-forgetfulness" to be helpful and bring clarity. Have you ever tried to have a conversation with someone who continually re-directed the conversation back to their opinion or experience? Certainly all of us can be guilty of this at some point, but it can be exasperating to deal with someone who constantly does it, so every conversation revolves completely around them. While we may be better at conversation than this type of person, we can be guilty of the same thing in other areas of life. We are, in essence, trapped by ourselves and do not have the freedom of self-forgetfulness.

In a booklet entitled *The Freedom of Self-Forgetfulness*, Keller expounds on 1 Corinthians 3:21 to 4:7 written by the apostle Paul. Paul reaches a point in his Christian life where he is simply not fixated on himself anymore. Keller states that "the essence of gospel-humility is not thinking more of myself or thinking less of myself, it is thinking of myself less."[70] Christian humility can be inaccurately perceived as self-deprecation or walking around with a cloud of condemnation on your head. No, that is definitely not it! Rather, it is when we no longer need to connect every experience back to our self. It is the freedom of self-forgetfulness that Paul found in Christ. It is an ego that is not puffed up but filled up with Christ.

> Christ must increase and we must decrease (John 3:30).

Keller goes on to say: "Are we talking about high self-esteem? No. So is it low self-esteem? Certainly not. It is not about self-esteem. Paul simply refuses to play that game...and that is the secret."[71] It is not about making false dichotomies where we must either love ourselves or hate ourselves. As John the Baptist aptly worded it, Christ must increase and we must decrease (John 3:30), and in each of our lives that will look a little different.

Questions for Reflection and Discussion

1. Did you have an inaccurate view of Christian humility or biblical self-image? How did this chapter bring clarity?
2. Read Galatians 6:8 and Romans 8:5-6. What we "feed" in our life will grow. How can you better feed your spiritual life? What in your life is feeding your innate self-absorption?

3. "God accepts me because_____." What are some ways that we can be tempted to finish this sentence? Why are we accepted?

4. Does self-denial mean that we can never say no to someone or enjoy personal interests in life?

Chapter 8

Living in Light of the Gospel

Revival occurs when those who think they already know the
gospel discover they do not fully know it. —Timothy Keller

Preaching the gospel to ourselves every day addresses both
the self-righteous Pharisee and the guilt-laden sinner
that dwell in our hearts. —Jerry Bridges

In the opening years of the twentieth century, New Thought laid
down a cultural precedent which eventually influenced Christianity.
As early as the 1920's, psychological concepts began to blend with
biblical truth, primarily in mainline protestant churches. Faith
began to be perceived as a source of self-improvement. The stage
was set for the very likable Norman Vincent Peale to bring it to
the masses. While it took longer to invade evangelical circles, it did
eventually weave its way in.

We can observe its influence in various ways. For instance, the
Bible can be perceived like a "how to" manual with tips for living
a good life or solving problems. This may not be explicitly stated,
but it is the clear underlying perspective. Consider sermons with
titles such as "5 ways to win over worry" or "3 secrets of a better

marriage." An extensive biography on Norman Vincent Peale is entitled *God's Salesman*. The title captures a core concern about this approach—it is about selling the benefits of a product named "God." Instead of proclaiming "Jesus Christ and him crucified" (1 Corinthians 2:2), we are giving out good advice about improving our lives. This creates people who are consumed with their own well-being, and it diverts them from Christ.

In John 5, Jesus rebukes the religious leaders of his day because they diligently studied the Scriptures to find eternal life but failed to see Jesus in them (verses 39-40). They missed the point, and we can easily miss the point too. Many lives have been transformed by Christ, thus faith can be a source of improvement. But it is not self-improvement, and Christianity cannot be based on a model of self-improvement. That is not what it is all about. *The Christian faith is about Christ.* Glenn Kreider points out that:

> To study the Scriptures without recognizing their proper aim is to misread them....Since the Scriptures testify about Jesus, any reading that fails to hear Jesus, any interpretation that fails to elevate Jesus, and any Bible study that fails to focus on Jesus is incorrect and worthy of judgment.[72]

Focusing on self-improvement feeds our natural weakness towards pride and self-sufficiency which only makes it more difficult for us to see our need of a Savior. The essence of Christianity is death of self, a new birth (John 3) into a new way of living based upon our relationship with Jesus Christ, and the on-going work of the Holy Spirit in our life.

A different but related issue is the large emphasis in the church on the "doing" side of faith: the importance of serving and using our gifts. We are urged not to be "pew-sitters." Our faith should certainly be active, but our motivations can be neglected. The emphasis is on "what to do" without a corresponding focus on the "why" or the underlying beliefs about God. What is driving us? We need to prioritize what the biblical text teaches us about our Savior, and approach the Bible with a God-ward focus rather than a self-ward one.

Doctrine Matters

When learning a vocation in college, theory is studied along with practice. Someone can be taught a skill alone, but without the theory behind it, the person will lack critical thinking and trouble-shooting ability. Such a person could prove dangerous especially in certain professions. In the church there can be a bypassing of "theory"—a neglect of doctrine or theology. Words like theory, doctrine, and theology can have negative connotations and are sometimes considered irrelevant, yet it is doctrine that provides the "why" behind what we do and provides the proper motivation and power to live our faith. Avoiding doctrine is like trying to build a house without a proper foundation. The way we live our faith can become warped and even cause damage when it is built on an inadequate biblical groundwork.

> The gospel is relegated to the proverbial shelf...how can this be?

In the Reformation, the doctrine of justification was paramount. In modern times, the focus shifted to sanctification. Far too often, the gospel is relegated to the proverbial shelf after the initial salvation experience. We don't need it anymore because we have moved on to sanctification; we are busy living our Christian life. We understand the gospel as a message primarily for unbelievers, thus we neglect Christ and his great salvation...unless there are unbelievers in the vicinity. How can this be?

It is true in one respect that the gospel is simple, and even a child or someone with limited mental capacity can understand the basics of salvation though Christ: We are sinful and fall short of God's holy perfection. We deserve punishment and eternal separation from God. God lived a human life as Jesus Christ, and Jesus became our substitute by taking our punishment for us when he died on the cross. Through faith in the death and resurrection of Jesus from the dead, we can have forgiveness of our sin and a restored relationship with God. We can over-complicate this simple message. No one needs a class in soteriology to become a Christian.

Yet, the gospel is also profound. God was crucified for us. That is mind-boggling! We can never exhaust its riches and implications. The cross of Christ is the most significant and glorious work in human history. If we have truly grasped this fact, we will never "move on" from it but will only seek to grow deeper in our understanding of it. As proclaimed in Romans 11:33: "Oh, the depth of the riches of the wisdom and knowledge of God! How unsearchable his judgments, and his paths beyond tracing out!"

Salvation and sanctification are each a side of the same coin. They go together. Our sanctification flows from our justification, but our methodologies do not make this clear. We want people to obey God's commands, but we do not give them a foundation on which to do so. Second Corinthians 5:21 states, "God made him [Jesus] who had no sin to be sin for us, so that in him we might become the righteousness of God." It is *in him* we become righteous. The first step in obedience is not "do" but believe.

If our obedience is not springing forth from our position in Christ, we can end up doing good things in the wrong spirit and with wrong motivations. As addressed in chapter 2, we can easily drift into self-righteousness or legalistic pride. Christians need to hear the gospel as much as non-Christians.

The epistles of Paul in the New Testament are primarily directed to believers, whether churches or individual Christians.

Does this mean Paul did not write about Christ and salvation much? *Hardly!* "With Paul, doctrine and duty go together. Doctrine is the basis for duty. Duty is the result of doctrine."[73] As in Ephesians 1-3, Colossians 1-2, and Romans 1-11, the openings of Paul's letters often begin with doctrine or a review of the truths of the gospel of Jesus Christ. Then Paul moves into "practical" content with instructions and exhortations about living the Christian life—based on who Christ is and what he has done. I put practical in quotes, because doctrine is practical content too. We should not dichotomize them.

Declared Righteous

Sadly, teaching in general has fallen by the way side in too many churches, and the study of God and church nomenclature has become passé. Christians no longer know the words that explain exactly what they believe. Justification is one of the most important Christian doctrines, yet many believers have little understanding of it. Maybe you learned in Sunday school as a child that justification means "just as if I never sinned." The play on words can help us remember it, but it is an *incomplete* definition. A fuller understanding of justification can eliminate a variety of faulty beliefs and attitudes that can hinder us in the Christian life. Let's consider justification and demonstrate how very relevant it is for the believer.

The word justification is not typically used in modern language, but its derivatives are. We may say that we were justified in doing something, meaning we had a right reason for it. Or we might say a court decision was just, meaning that justice was done. This inches us in the direction of biblical justification.

Justification is expounded upon particularly in Romans, and refers to the fact that the person who comes to Christ in faith is declared righteous in the sight of God. It is not mere pardon or forgiveness, which is where "just as if I never sinned" falls short. Pardon or forgiveness is "negative" in that it removes something. The person is still guilty, but the punishment or debt has been waved. The burden of our sin was transferred to the cross of Christ, and the sinless Son of God took the penalty for our sin upon himself. Truly, we have been forgiven in Christ, but justification goes beyond this.

Justification is "positive" in that it adds something to us. An astonishing "exchange" takes place: not only did Christ bear our sin, but we also gain his righteousness. It is a judicial act where the righteousness of Christ is credited to us. Romans 3:21-24 asserts:

> But now apart from the law the righteousness of God has been made known...This righteousness is given through faith in Jesus Christ to all who believe...and all are justified freely by his grace through the redemption that came by Christ Jesus.

Such wonderful words: given, freely, grace. Our justification is by grace through faith, and not by keeping the law. Grace is the undeserved kindness of God, and we cannot earn it or deserve it. Romans 3:25-26 goes on to say that God through Christ is *both* the just one and the justifier of those who have faith in Jesus. It is not about our work but the work of Jesus for us. Our attempts at righteousness will always fall short; therefore we must trust in the righteousness of Christ. I appreciated this explanation:

> It [justification] does not mean the believer becomes sinless or righteous in himself. Rather, God...covers him with a robe of righteousness. God now sees him as being in Christ and he is accepted, not because of who he is, but because of Christ's person and work.[74]

Romans 5:1-11 affirms the benefits we possess "since we have been justified through faith." Peace and reconciliation with God are ours through our Lord Jesus Christ. We have hope even in suffering and salvation from God's future wrath. The verdict has been announced ahead of time! We are not condemned, and the verdict on judgment day is that we will be counted righteous because the righteousness of Christ became ours through faith. No matter what our circumstances in life, we have security in Christ.

If you have never studied or carefully read through the book of Romans, I highly encourage you to do so. You will gain a deeper understanding of the many facets of our wondrous salvation and all that was accomplished for us in Jesus Christ. John Stott, in his commentary on Romans, provides this summary of our great salvation:

> Faith's only function is to receive what grace offers.
> —John Stott

> Justification...is the heart of the gospel and unique to Christianity. No other system, ideology, or religion proclaims free forgiveness...On the contrary, all other systems teach some form of self-salvation through good works...Christianity, by contrast, is not in its essence a religion at all; it is a gospel, the gospel, good news that God's grace has turned away his wrath, that God's Son has died our death and borne our judgment, that God has mercy on the undeserving, and that there is nothing left for us to do, or even contribute. Faith's only function is to receive what grace offers.[75]

So...how does this help us live the Christian life? We enter the life of faith this way, but how can it guide us in our daily living?

Keep Living by Grace

We begin the Christian life by grace through faith, yet we can easily regress into a performance or works based relationship with God. We have a theoretical commitment to justification, but our day-to-day life reveals that we rely on our sanctification or at least have a preoccupation with it. This is not surprising because grace goes against our natural instincts, and we are prone to turn inward. We prefer to earn—and therefore deserve—what we get in life, and this is precisely why we need to continually remind ourselves of gospel truths.

We can too easily become captive to criticism or praise from other people and end up living for their approval. Worse yet, we can think we are living for approval or favor from God. Some Christians live as though Christianity is based on the concepts of karma and samsara from Hinduism where your past actions (whether bad or good) determine your destiny. No, the Christian message is radically different!

In Christianity we do not get what we deserve because Jesus bore the penalty for us. Our bad behavior does not condemn us, and our good behavior does not gain us God's favor. Read the second half of that sentence again. Our good behavior could not gain us salvation (Ephesians 2:8-9), so why do we think it can gain us favor after salvation? We already have God's favor!

We passed from death to life (John 5:24) when we came to Christ in faith. The book of Ephesians uses the phrase "in Christ" and emphasizes the spiritual riches we possess in him. Romans 5:2 says that through Christ "we have gained access by faith into this grace in which we now stand." Are we standing in grace, in God's undeserved favor? Or are we standing in our own righteousness, looking for favor? John 1:16-17 reminds us that while the law came through Moses, grace and truth came through Jesus Christ. Through Jesus it is grace upon grace—one gracious gift after another.

Galatians 6:14 says, "May I never boast except in the cross of our Lord Jesus Christ." That means we are not boasting in or trusting in our moral behavior. Besides, how can we trump what Jesus did for us? We can never come close! Rest in the tremendous favor you possess because of what Christ did for you. Reminding ourselves of the gospel grounds us in humility and directs us away from our inherent self-absorption. We need to "be found in him, not having a righteousness of our own that comes from the law, but that which is through faith in Christ, the righteousness that comes from God on the basis of faith" (Philippians 3:9). It doesn't get clearer than that, my friends.

> Rest in the tremendous favor you possess because of what Christ did for you.

A Radical New Dynamic for Living

Our justification is not merely a past event, but a present and future reality, and we should be living in light of it. It should give us a radical new dynamic for living which can prevent us from drifting into either self-delusion or self-condemnation. We were declared righteous by grace through faith and it was not based on our behavior, so why should we now become either deluded or condemned? Our identity is secure in Christ. When we fully understand our secure position based upon the righteousness of Christ, it gives us a confident foundation for living.

Christians can fail to be honest about their sin. Instead of admitting our sin to ourselves or to other believers, we keep it secret. We live in a state of self-delusion. We do not pray like David for God to search us, know our heart, and reveal our sin (Psalm 139:23-24). As chapter 3 emphasized, a light view of sin makes light of the sacrifice Jesus made for us. Living in light of our justification frees us to be honest with ourselves. We can face our sin, and only when sin is faced is there any hope of conquering it.

Fear of condemnation is one reason we may be in denial about our sin. Perhaps when we faced our sin in the past, we felt defeated, despaired, or beat ourselves up. Again, it is a symptom that we are not living in light of our justification. Romans 8:1 boldly proclaims that there is no condemnation for those who are in Christ Jesus. No condemnation! Our identity is in Christ, not our behavior. We could not earn or deserve our salvation in the first place, consequently how could we "un-earn" it? Please do not misunderstand—sin can create serious and even devastating consequences in this life—but we are not condemned because of it. We can fall into the arms of our gracious Savior, ask forgiveness, grow wiser, and move forward in our Christian life. The final verses of Romans 8 give us the reassuring words that nothing, absolutely nothing, can separate us from the love of God. *Not even ourselves.*

The concept of free grace, along with its absolute security and lack of condemnation, makes some people nervous because they fear it can be taken advantage of and used as a license to sin. That concern is nothing new, and the apostle Paul had to address it himself. As he said in Romans 6:1-2, "Shall we go on sinning so that grace may increase? By no means!"

Some will use the derogatory phrase "easy believism." It is true that the gospel can be presented in a faulty manner. However, there is really no such thing as easy believism. We are asking someone to believe that God became a human two thousand ago, died a horrific death, and then came back to life. Think about that as an outsider instead of someone who has heard it most of your life. Paul said in 1 Corinthians 1:23 that "we preach Christ crucified: a *stumbling block* to Jews and *foolishness* to Gentiles" [emphasis added]. I've had students from multiple countries and religions live with me, and several had little familiarity with Christianity. I had the privilege of explaining the basics to them, but it was *outlandish* to their ears.

There is nothing easy about grace either. Well, grace is easy, but that is what makes it difficult. It's too easy. All we must do is admit our need, and believe. It can be terribly hard for people to admit they are helpless, sinful, and need a Savior. We consider ourselves good and expect that God should accept our efforts. We want to do it ourselves instead of throwing ourselves on his mercy.

We must not forget that grace was very costly to God. In Luke 23:43, Jesus told the criminal next to him: "Truly I tell you, today you will be with me in paradise." Consider the scene: Jesus is on the cross. The criminal believed. He received free salvation as Jesus was paying for that salvation by giving his life.

If a person really grasps the truths of the gospel and believes it, this changes everything. How can they ever be the same again? We are recipients of *amazing* grace! Undeserved kindness was lavished upon us. When we are living in light of our justification, it helps provide proper motivation for living the Christian life. We are not living *for* approval from God, but *from* approval from God.[76] The purest motivation for Christian conduct comes from what God has done for us. We obey our Savior from a grateful heart. Titus 2:11-14 says that our response to the grace of God should be to say "no" to ungodliness and worldly passions. Perhaps the problem is that we are preaching grace far too little, rather than too much! We should celebrate the kindness of God, and make choices in life that reflect the reality of grace.

In contrast, methods are used that utilize pressure, fear, or guilt to motivate people. We hold up God's commands as an expectation and raise the bar high. We make God's way seem burdensome, but God's way is not supposed to be a burden but a joy. Jesus said that his yoke is easy and his burden light, and he pronounced "woe" on the Pharisees because they placed unbearable religious demands on people (Matthew 11:30; 23:4). We are supposed to run the race of faith like Christ did, for the joy set before him, and not with fear, guilt, and pressure chasing us down.

Telling people they must love does not necessarily create love. It can backfire, and people may do what they are supposed to do with an unloving spirit or a sense of obligation alone. Have you ever been on the receiving end of an unloving, obligatory deed? I have. It is not pleasant. Pressure or guilt can bring short-term behavioral change, but rarely does it lead to genuine transformation of the heart that brings lasting change.

First John 4:19 says that we love *because* Jesus first loved us. The apostle Paul said that the love of Christ compelled or controlled him (2 Corinthians 5:14). Our motivation should arise out of an awareness of the tremendous grace, mercy, love, and forgiveness demonstrated towards us in Christ. Point people to Christ, and help them to comprehend his great love.

In Luke 7 we read the story of a sinful woman who came to see Jesus when he was eating in the home of a Pharisee. This woman wept before Jesus, anointed his feet with precious oil, and wiped his feet with her hair. The Pharisee was inwardly disturbed that Jesus let this sinful woman touch him in this brash way, yet the Pharisee had not offered even the common courtesy of foot washing to Jesus. Jesus then told a brief parable revealing that because this woman was forgiven of much sin, she loved much. It should be the same for us. If we are truly aware of our great sinfulness and the great forgiveness we found in Jesus, it should overwhelm us with love for Jesus and other people. Jesus said if we love him, we will keep his commandments (John 14:21). Is the love of Christ compelling us?

A brief book I highly recommend to you is *A Gospel Primer for Christians* by Milton Vincent. As the title indicates, the author takes the truths of the gospel and presents them for the Christian reader. It is permeated with Scripture, captures the essence of the gospel in a straightforward way, and reminds us of why we need the gospel every day. We must never put the gospel on the shelf. We must never let it become familiar, stale, or ordinary to us. It must become woven into our hearts and minds so that it reshapes our perspectives and become the lens through which we view all of life.

Questions for Reflection and Discussion

1. Have you tended to approach the Bible primarily looking for advice on living your life? Why is this problematic?
2. The old hymn states "My hope is built on nothing less than Jesus' blood and righteousness." What other things are we tempted to build our hopes on?
3. Why are we so prone to turn to our good deeds—whether before or after salvation? What sin is at the root of this?
4. Look up Romans 3:20-28; 4:4-5; 5:1-2 and 8:33. How would you define justification in your own words?
5. Carefully read through Ephesians chapters 1 and 2. Record all the blessings we possess because of what Christ did for us. Share what is most significant to you and why.
6. Have you been more likely to drift into self-delusion or self-condemnation? If we live in light of our justification, how does it keep us from these extremes?
7. Some fear that an emphasis on grace will lead to sinful living. How could you answer this concern?
8. Are you confident that God has justified you, declared you righteous, in his sight? Do you know when this happened in your life? If you have never placed your faith in the Lord Jesus Christ, I urge you to do so. You can do it now. Simply pray. Ask for forgiveness of your sin, and place your confidence in what Jesus did for you in his life, death, and resurrection. If you have questions, please speak with a Christian in your life or a church leader who can further explain the gospel to you.

Chapter 9

Gospel-Immersed Community

Are humility and honest confession characteristic of our churches? Not much of the time. Increasingly common is the self-assured, goal-oriented, achievement-driven, human-centered outlook. What would the evangelistic impact be if the popular profile of today's Christian emphasized sin and brokenness…
—Peter Nelson

What embitters the world is not excess of criticism, but an absence of self-criticism. —G.K. Chesterton

The positive thinking movement that overcame our culture influenced the life of the believer *within* the church, and this affected the believer when outside the church. While evangelicals can have a positive reputation for humanitarian work in their communities, unfortunately we can also have a negative reputation for being judgmental, holier-than-thou, hypocritical, and lacking in grace. We can be moral crusaders who target certain sins in others while overlooking sin in our own lives. Humility is not a practiced virtue among us. While evangelicals can be unfairly maligned, we need to admit there is some accuracy and truth in these accusations.

115

John 15 contains the well-known "Jesus is the vine, we are the branches" passage. This passage must be set in its chapter context to fully understand its breadth and depth. One way to outline John 15 is this: verses 1-11: abide in Christ, verses 12-17: love believers, and verses 18-27: witness in the world. As Christians, we should have relationships with Christ, other believers, and the world. The order is critical and they are linked together. Abiding in Christ is foremost, and it determines our effectiveness in loving other believers. If we are effective in our witness in the world, it is because we have *first* been abiding in Christ and loving believers. While not neglecting the core of abiding in Christ, what I want to focus on in this chapter is our relationship with other believers. Our fellowship with the believers in our local church sets the pattern for the relationships we will build outside the church.

Socializing Versus Fellowship

Our relationships with other believers can be tragically shallow. Even small groups or Sunday school classes can be more like superficial social clubs. This can't be blamed on one thing alone. Our fast-paced modern world makes it hard to slow down and invest in each other. The positive thinking mentality exploited our sinful weakness towards self-reliance and pride. There is also a rampant misuse or misunderstanding of the word fellowship in the church. Socialization and fellowship are confused. They are not the same thing. Donald Whitney, in his book on the spiritual disciplines, clarifies for us:

> Although socializing is often both a part of and the context of fellowship, it is possible to socialize without having fellowship. Socializing involves the sharing of human and earthly life. Christian

fellowship, New Testament *koinonia*, involves the sharing of spiritual life. Don't misunderstand— socializing is a valuable asset to the church and necessary for a balanced life. But we have gone beyond giving socializing the place it deserves. We have become willing to accept it as a substitute for fellowship, almost cheating ourselves of the Christian birthright of true fellowship altogether.[77]

There is a distinction between sharing earthly life and spiritual life. Are we sharing spiritual life? Secular community groups, such as a bowling league or billiards team, can socialize and assist each other in times of need or crisis in life. Does this mean they are a church? Of course not. Christians should go beyond this with each other and be sharing the spiritual life. We are the body of Christ and possess the Holy Spirit. Multiple verses tell us to love one another. We are also told to:

- Motivate one another towards love and good deeds (Hebrews 10:24)
- Confess our sins to one another, pray for one another (James 5:16)
- Accept one another, be patient and humble with one another, forgive one another (Romans 15:7; Ephesians 4:2; Colossians 3:13)
- Encourage one another so we are not deceived by sin (Hebrews 3:13)
- Teach and admonish one another with Godly wisdom and Scripture (Colossians 3:16; 1 Thessalonians 4:18)
- Submit to one another (Ephesians 5:21)
- Serve one another with our spiritual gifts (1 Peter 4:10)

There are even more one-anothers! As believers, we are called to initiate involvement in each other's lives. How are we doing with our spiritual one-anothering?

Many of the one-another statements involve being honest and authentic with each other, which requires humility. We must be humble enough to confess our sin and have a willingness to learn from others. We are to forgive each other, which presupposes that there will be indiscretions to forgive as we experience life together. Are we praying for each other's spiritual growth, or are we only praying for physical needs? Consider the powerful spiritual prayers of the apostle Paul for his fellow believers in Colossians 1:9-14 and Ephesians 3:14-21. Do our gatherings reflect an atmosphere of honest confession, prayer, humility, and dependence on God? Ultimately our gathering should reflect Christ as Philippians 2:5-8 states:

> In your relationships with one another,
> have the same mindset as Christ Jesus:
>
> Who, being in very nature God,
> did not consider equality with God
> something to be used to his own advantage;
> rather, he made himself nothing
> by taking the very nature of a servant,
> being made in human likeness.
> And being found in appearance as a man,
> he humbled himself
> by becoming obedient to death—
> even death on a cross!

Previously in the chapter, I said that our fellowship with other believers sets the pattern for the relationships we will build outside the church. Do you see the problem here? If we are not learning to be authentic people of grace and humility among ourselves, it is no wonder that we go out into the community and can have reputations as holier-than-thou hypocrites lacking grace.

Christians need deep and genuine relationships with each other. Just being together is not enough. We must humbly realize how much we need each other, and participate rather than just show up. Positive thinking has contributed to an individualistic perception of faith, as though the gospel pertains to individuals alone. But the gospel has purified a people for Christ (Titus 2:14), and as people, we are made for community. Ephesians 4:14 says that we do not want to be spiritual infants who lack discernment and are tossed about by false philosophies or teachings. Instead,

> speaking the truth in love, we will grow to become in every respect the mature body of him who is the head, that is, Christ. From him the whole body, joined and held together by every supporting ligament, grows and builds itself up in love, as each part does its work. (Ephesians 4:15-16)

We need each other in order to grow in the likeness of Jesus. Sometimes we must speak the truth in love when there are false ideas. Each part of the body plays a critical role, and no one is dispensable or unimportant.

No Golden Age for the Church

However, we do need a realistic view of the church. We will be disappointed, let down, and even hurt by people in the fellowship. As Flannery O'Conner said to someone, "All your dissatisfactions with the church seem to me to come from an incomplete understanding of sin....Christianity makes a difference; but it cannot kill the age."[78] We are all works in progress, saints and sinners, making our way towards the Celestial City. We are a mixed bunch in different stages of spiritual understanding and growth. People begin their Christian journey with different types of baggage. You may think a certain person is lacking in spiritual progress, yet if you only knew their background, you'd realize they have actually made tremendous progress.

> Christianity makes a difference; but it cannot kill the age.
> —Flannery O'Conner

There has never been a golden age for the church. Read the New Testament and church history. From the book of Acts onward in the New Testament, we see a church that had struggles, disagreements, and sin in the camp. The early church was not a glowing tale of non-stop triumph and perfection. So why would we expect that now? Individual people of God in both the Old and New Testament struggled with sin. Abraham lied. Jacob was a deceiver. David was an adulterer and a murderer. Impetuous Peter put his foot in his mouth and denied his Savior. Ananias and Sapphira were deceptive with money. Paul and Barnabas quarreled about a ministry partner. Again, you may wonder the point here. Am I trying to be discouraging? No. The voice of reality can actually prevent us from becoming discouraged and disillusioned. As Stephen Mansfield says in his book *ReChurch*, written for people who have experienced very real hurt in the church:

> It is our naïveté, the sentimental gloss we put over the world that leads us to folly and hurt. To know the gritty truth about life straight from the pages of Scripture is part of the grace of God and allows us to live safely and effectively in a fallen world.[79]

When we have a realistic view of ourselves and each other, we can experience freedom. Instead of being trapped by false delusions, we can learn to accept each other and live in light of the grace by which we were saved. Are we living in light of our justification? We don't have to pretend to be people we are not, but we are free to admit our doubts, spiritual struggles, and sin to God and each other.

I think we have all heard the disheartening story of a Christian who, to everyone's shock, was found to be involved in a moral scandal or suddenly rejected Christian faith. No one was aware of the turmoil brewing behind the scenes, and that is precisely the problem. Our gatherings do not typically reflect an atmosphere of honest confession, prayer, humility, and dependence on God— places where a Christian struggling with sins or doubts can share them and seek support. Instead, the problem hides, grows in secret, and suddenly erupts.

Walk in the Light

Sin wants to remain unknown because that is when it is most powerful over a person. As the book of 1 John emphasizes, we need to be walking in the light. Light has revelatory function, but darkness keeps things hidden. Remember the relationship of sin to pride and self-deception. When we try to hide what we are, we walk in the dark. First John 1:7-10 states:

> But if we walk in the light, as he [Jesus] is in the light, we have fellowship with one another, and the blood of Jesus, his Son, purifies us from all sin. If we claim to be without sin, we deceive ourselves and the truth is not in us. If we confess our sins, he is faithful and just and will forgive us our sins and purify us from all unrighteousness. If we claim we

have not sinned, we make him out to be a liar and
his word is not in us.

The basis for fellowship with God and with each other is open
exposure, not cowering in the dark. When we stop pretending with
God and each other, the fellowship has a chance of becoming a
true unity of believers where sin can be dealt with and conquered
through the blood of Jesus. Yet too many of us prefer to live in the
dark. As Dietrich Bonhoeffer states in *Life Together*:

> The pious fellowship permits no one to be a sinner.
> So everybody must conceal his sin from himself
> and from the fellowship. We dare not be sinners.
> Many Christians are unthinkably horrified when a
> real sinner is suddenly discovered among the
> righteous. So we remain alone with our sin, living
> in lies and hypocrisy. The fact is that we *are* sinners![80]

> The basis for fellowship...
> is open exposure, not
> cowering in the dark.

I hope this chapter serves as a
review of the previous content of
the book, and helps bring it to a
conclusion. Can you see why pride
is a beast most savage? Why sin
must not be evaded? Why we need a biblically balanced Christianity
remembering that we are saints and sinners living in the already but
not yet? Why the way up is down in Christianity? Why we must live
in light of the gospel and keep ourselves immersed in gospel truths?
It all applies here. The sham must end. We can't hide anything from
God, and true liberation can come when we live in light of the life,
death, and resurrection of our Lord Jesus.

Hebrews 3:13 says we should encourage each other *so that* we
are not hardened by sin's deceitfulness. We need each other so that
the effects of sin are counteracted by the involvement of our sisters

and brothers in Christ. I once heard it said that our self-perception is about as accurate as one of those carnival mirrors. Other people can see us more clearly, and we need them to lovingly speak into our life with counsel.

Galatians 6:2 contains a well-known phrase: bear (or carry) each other's burdens. I've often seen this phrase taken out of context to refer to practical assistance in a time of need, like delivering a home-cooked meal. Of course, we should help each other in this way, but in context, this verse is about the burden of temptation and sin in our lives. Galatians chapter 5 is about the conflict of the flesh and Spirit and the different fruit they bring forth in our life. Chapter 6 begins by describing the gentle restoration of a person who has been caught in sin. Then we reach verse 2 about bearing each other's burdens. Context brings clarity. Verse 3 goes on to say that, "If anyone thinks they are something when they are not, they deceive themselves." Being a burden-bearer requires humility of both the restorer and the restored. We cannot be "unthinkably horrified" by sin among us. We must realize we are sinners too, and not think of ourselves above similar spiritual failure.

All this sounds good in theory, but is hard to initiate in our real-life fellowships. We can lead by example, and that will require both courage and humility. We risk being misunderstood or perceived as holier-than-thou when we attempt to move the group into a deeper spiritual dynamic. People can be uncomfortable when you openly share sin or struggles. I've experienced this first hand. Once in a small group, I shared how I'd been feeling vengeful and vindictive towards someone who wronged me. The leader looked at me with a dumbfounded expression and made a nervous joke about not wanting to get on my bad side. The rest of the group was clearly uneasy and seemed surprised that a Christian would admit to these things. I found out at a later time that the leader of this group was having a terrible struggle with one of his young adult children, but never shared this with us. I thought that if we'd only known, we could have offered prayerful support.

To move a group in an authentic direction will likely require both a leader and a participant or two who have a humble heart's desire to do so. Much behind the scenes prayer is essential, and a conducive environment is necessary. We need to develop trust with others, which takes time. Caution and discretion is required; some things may best be shared one-on-one rather than with a group. Yet we must improve our ability to create atmospheres that emanate authenticity, humility, and honesty. We must stop settling for socialization and *cheating ourselves of the Christian birthright of true fellowship.* I feel that prayer and leading by example are the best routes to take. Pounding away on the importance of authentic community will not work. As this statement clarifies:

> I tend to notice that when people use the words authenticity and community a lot, both tend to leave the premises. It's easy to use authenticity and community as new marketing tools to win customers to our product; as soon as that happens, we violate authenticity and community. I think we get closer to both by pursuing love —by practicing the virtues found in 1 Corinthians 13.[81]

We create community by loving each other. When community in and of itself is the focus, the authentic community we seek can remain evasive and just out of reach. Christ must be the focus, and community should flow from a commitment to him. Is the love of Christ controlling us? We cannot "do" community but must "be" a community that reflects Christ.

I know Christians who are desperate to experience true fellowship with other believers and are discouraged at their inability to find it. Others may have no idea what they are missing, having never experienced true Christian fellowship. It may need to begin with you and just one other person. Begin to meet together, drop the masks, and pray for each other spiritually. Pray that another person might eventually join you, and who knows where God might lead it. Humility and honest confession must become a characteristic of our individual lives and our churches. This would tremendously help our evangelistic witness in this world. When we, the messengers, better reflect our humble Savior and emanate his grace, our tarnished reputations will begin to be repaired.

Questions for Reflection and Discussion

1. Had you confused socialization and fellowship?
2. Why is insincerity so destructive to Christian relationships?
3. What is your greatest fear or reluctance about sharing spiritual needs and sin struggles with other believers?

Concluding Thoughts

The positive thinking movement undermined Christianity in subtle ways, but subtle things can be more damaging and destructive than the blatant. They sneak up on us and alter our perspectives unawares. When the church came under the power of this movement, it had the significant consequence of distracting us from Christ, shifting our priorities, and creating a different gospel entirely: the "positivity gospel." I hope this book will help reorient your thinking to see all of life through the gospel of Jesus Christ. As 1 Corinthians 1:18 proclaims, "the message of the cross is foolishness to those who are perishing, but to us who are being saved it is the power of God."

I urge you to exercise caution and critical thinking with Christian books and sermons to which you expose yourself. Are they turning your eyes upon Jesus, or feeding your innate self-absorption? We matter in life, but Jesus is the point. When our thoughts are fixed upon HIM, it gives us the proper foundation and power source from which to live our lives. Please see the appendix for practical ideas and resources.

Appendix of practical ideas and resources for cultivating humility and staying focused on Christ

➤ Pray with the Psalmist: "Search me, God, and know my heart; test me and know my anxious thoughts. See if there is any offensive way in me, and lead me in the way everlasting." (Psalm 139:23-24)

➤ Sing, listen to, or contemplate songs with a distinct focus on the gospel. Look for songs with deeper depth of content. Music tastes differ, but here are some songs that I appreciate:

"My Hope is Built on Nothing Less" by Edward Mote, 1834. (Or Hillsong United's contemporary version of it entitled "Cornerstone.")

"One Day" by J. Wilber Chapman, 1911. (Or Casting Crown's contemporary version of it entitled "Glorious Day.")

"Jesus Paid it All" by Elvina Hall, 1865. (Or Kristian Stanfill's contemporary version.)

"I Will Sing of My Redeemer" by Philip Bliss, 1876.

"Hallelujah, What a Savior" by Philip Bliss, 1875.

"Marvelous Grace of Our Loving Lord" by Julia Johnston, 1911.

"Jesus, Messiah" by Chris Tomlin.

If you are not familiar with modern-day hymn writers Keith and Kristyn Getty, explore their worthwhile music: www. gettymusic.com.

Indelible Grace Music helps "the church recover the tradition of putting old hymns to new music for each generation, and to enrich our worship with a huge view of God and His indelible grace." www.igracemusic.com

➤ Consider the majestic greatness of God. Read and ponder passages such as: Job 38-42; Psalm 8, 93, 104, 145; Isaiah 40; Revelation 4-5. Pray to be really gripped by God's greatness.

➤ Memorize or contemplate Bible verses about the gospel. Keep the verses accessible to your sight. Write them on notecards to place on a mirror, visor, or in your pocket. Verses or passages to consider: 2 Corinthians 5:21; Hebrews 12:1-2; 1 Corinthians 15:3-4; Galatians 2:20-21; Romans 3:23-24; Romans 5:1-11 or any verses in that section such as verse 1-2 or 6-8, Philippians 2:1-11, Philippians 3:8-9.

In our modern technological age, you can easily view these verses on your phone. Why bother writing them down? There is something more personal and tangible about handwriting that can help content become a part of you, and scientific studies are revealing the benefits of this.

Memorizing Scripture can be difficult. Rather than memorizing directly, take an indirect approach to become familiar with the verses. For example, camp out in Romans chapters 3-5 for a while. Read through these chapters multiple times over the course of a month. Read quickly to get the big picture. Read slowly to pick up on details. Reflect or meditate on certain verses. Pray specific verses. Read through some Bible commentaries on these chapters. After immersing yourself like this, you will find that you have almost memorized some of the content, or it has at least become a part of you in a whole new way.

➤ The following books have been helpful to me related to topics such as humility, holiness, sin, grace, and the gospel. They reflect a variety of writing styles from devotional to academic.

Knowing God by JI Packer
Books by Jerry Bridges, such as: *The Pursuit of Holiness, The Discipline of Grace, The Transforming Power of the Gospel*
Why Sin Matters by Mark R. McMinn
Humility by Andrew Murray
The Ragamuffin Gospel by Brennan Manning
An Arrow Pointing to Heaven by James Bryan Smith (a devotional biography of Richard Mullins)
The Mortification of Sin by John Owen (edition with an introduction by JI Packer)
The Race Set Before Us by Thomas R. Schreiner & Ardel Caneday
The Grace of God by Andy Stanley
God With Us by Glenn R. Kreider
The Cross of Christ by John Stott

➤ Some ideas for cultivating humility in your life, in addition to contemplating the gospel itself:

- Take an interest in others. Reach out. Consider them more important than yourself.
- Realize you are not indispensable. Things will go on without you. Really, they will.
- Nurture thankfulness and practice gratitude (1 Thessalonians 5:18).
- Pray for it! Pray to be less self-absorbed. Pray that Christ will increase and you will decrease (John 3:30).

- Talk less and listen more (James 1:19; Proverbs 29:20).
- Make every effort to understand where the other person is coming from, even if you disagree on the issue.
- Accept correction or feedback from others graciously (Proverbs 10:17, 12:1). Even inaccurate or dubious feedback can have a kernel of truth we need to hear.
- Romans 12:15 instructs us to: "Rejoice with those who rejoice; mourn with those who mourn." I think we can be better at the later than the former. Rejoice and be genuinely pleased for others when they are promoted, honored, or attain a goal.
- Look for opportunities to serve others. Do what needs to be done. Lend a hand.
- Ask for help from others.
- Graciously accept a compliment with a thank you, but silently give glory to God (Galatians 6:14).
- Think of the person who irritates or annoys you as a means of grace to humble you.

This is certainly not an exhaustive list. Add your own. We are all different. Asking for help from others may seem like an odd or easy suggestion to you, but it can be very hard for self-sufficient (proud) people to ask for help.

➤ An excellent article with practical ideas on biblical fellowship is available online. "Cultivate Koinonia" by Donald Whitney. http://biblicalspirituality.org/wp-content/uploads/2011/01/Cultivate-Koinonia.pdf

Author contact

L.L. Martin can be contacted at:
positivelypowerless@gmail.com

L.L. Martin blogs at Enough Light.
"In faith there is enough light for those who want to believe
and enough shadows to blind those who don't." Blaise Pascal
https://lightenough.wordpress.com

Bibliography

Adams, Jay E. *The Biblical View of Self-Esteem, Self-Love, Self-Image.* Eugene: Harvest House, 1986.

Alsup, Wendy Horger. "Self-delusion Versus Self-condemnation." *Practical Theology for Women* website. October 20, 2011. http://www.theologyforwomen.org/2011/10/self-delusion-verses-self-condemnation.html

Alcorn, Randy. *If God is Good: Faith in the Midst of Suffering and Evil.* Colorado Springs: Multnomah Books, 2009.

Alter, Adam. "The Powerlessness of Positive Thinking." *The New Yorker,* February 13, 2014, accessed online: http://www.newyorker.com/business/currency/the-powerlessness-of-positive-thinking; Internet.

Bickel, Bruce and Stan Jantz. *World Religions & Cults.* Eugene: Harvest House, 2002.

Bonhoeffer, Dietrich. *Life Together.* San Francisco: Harper & Row, 1954.

Bridges, Jerry. *The Discipline of Grace.* Colorado Springs: NavPress, 1994.

Bridges, Jerry. *The Transforming Power of the Gospel.* Colorado Springs: NavPress, 2012.

Bridges, Jerry. *The Pursuit of Holiness.* Colorado Springs: NavPress, 1978.

Bruce, F.F. *The Epistle of Paul to the Romans.* Grand Rapids: Eerdmans Publishing, 1963.

Byrne, Rhonda. *The Secret.* New York: Atria Books, 2006.

Catron, James L.R., *New Testament Survey*. Dubuque: ECS Ministries, 2004.

Chambers, Oswald. *My Utmost for His Highest*. Uhrichsville, Ohio: Barbour, 1935/1963.

Chesterton, G.K. *Orthodoxy*. San Francisco: Ignatius Press, 1908.

Coleson, Joseph, ed. *Be Holy: God's Invitation to Understand, Declare, and Experience Holiness*. Indianapolis: Wesleyan Publishing House, 2008.

Constable, Thomas L. *Expository (Bible Study) Notes*. Available online: http://www.soniclight.com/constable/notes.htm

Douglas, JD, ed. *New Bible Dictionary*. Wheaton: Tyndale House, 1982.

Dyck, Drew. "How we Forgot the Holiness of God," *Christianity Today* 58, no. 4 (May 2014).

Dudley-Smith, Timothy, ed., *Authentic Christianity from the Writings of John Stott*. Downers Grove: InterVarsity Press, 1995.

Erickson, Millard J. *Introducing Christian Doctrine*. Grand Rapids: Baker Book House, 1992.

Frost, Michael. *Exiles: Living Missionally in a Post-Christian Culture*. Peabody: Hendrickson Publishers, 2006.

Fields, Leslie Leyland. "Throwing Christ over the Cliff." *Christianity Today* 56, no. 5 (May 2012): 50.

George, Carol V. R. *God's Salesman: Norman Vincent Peale and the Power of Positive Thinking*. New York: Oxford University Press, 1993.

Horowitz, Mitch. *One Simple Idea: How Positive Thinking Reshaped Modern Life*. New York: Crown Publishers, 2014.

Ironside, H.A. *Addresses on the Gospel of Luke*. New York: Loizeaux Brothers, 1946.

Janik, Erika. "Think Positive." *American History* Vol. 49, No. 1 (April 01, 2014): 50-57.

Jones, David W., and Russell S. Woodbridge. *Health, Wealth & Happiness: Has the Prosperity Gospel Overshadowed the Gospel of Christ?* Grand Rapids: Kregel Publications, 2011.

Keller, Timothy. *The Freedom of Self-forgetfulness*. Leyland, England: 10Publishing, 2012.

Keller, Timothy. *The Reason for God*. New York: Dutton, 2008.

Kreider, Glenn R. *God with Us: Exploring God's Personal Interactions with His People throughout the Bible*. Phillipsburg: P&R Publishing, 2014.

Koessler, John. "Jesus Disappoints Everyone." *Christianity Today* 56, no. 4 (April 2012), 44-47.

Konnikova, Maria. "Lessons from Sherlock Holmes: Confidence Is Good; Overconfidence, Not So Much." *Scientific American blog*. (September 6, 2011); accessed online: http://blogs. scientificamerican.com/guest-blog/2011/09/06/lessons-from-sherlock-holmes-confidence-is-good-overconfidence-not-so-much/; Internet.

Kullberg, Kelly Monroe and Lael Arrington, eds. *A Faith and Culture Devotional*. Grand Rapids: Zondervan, 2008.

Lewis, C.S. *Mere Christianity*. Old Tappen: Fleming Revell Company, 1952.

Lewis, C.S. *The Screwtape Letters*. New York: The MacMillan Company, 1962.

Lockyer, Herbert G. *The Sins of the Saints*. Neptune: Loizeaux Brothers, 1970.

Mahaney, C.J. *Living the Cross Centered Life*. Colorado Springs: Multnomah Books, 2006.

Macarthur, John. *The Vanishing Conscience*. Nelson Books, 1994/1995.

MacDonald, William. *Romans the Gospel of Grace*. Dubuque: Emmaus Bible College, 1970.

Manning, Brennan. *The Ragamuffin Gospel*. Colorado Springs: Multnomah Books, 1990/2000/2005.

Mansfield, Stephen. *ReChurch: Healing Your Way Back to the People of God*. Brentwood: BarnaBooks, 2010.

Martin, Walter. *The Kingdom of the Cults*. Minneapolis: Bethany House, 1985.

McDermott, Gerald R. *The Baker Pocket Guide to World Religions.* Grand Rapids: Baker Books, 2008.

McMinn, Mark R. *Why Sin Matters: The Surprising Relationship Between Our Sin and God's Grace.* Wheaton: Tyndale House, 2004.

Mulford, Prentice. *Thoughts are Things.* New York: Barnes & Noble, 1889/2007.

Murray, Andrew. *Humility.* (Updated edition) New Kensington: Whitaker House, 1982.

Nave, Orville J., ed. *Nave's Topical Bible.* Chicago: Moody Press, 1974.

Nelson, Peter K. "Impractical Christianity." *Christianity Today* 49, no. 9 (September 2005): 80-82.

Oden, Thomas C. *The Justification Reader.* Grand Rapids: Wm. B. Eerdmans Publishing, 2002.

Osteen, Joel. *Become a Better You.* New York: First Free Press, 2007.

Owen, John. *The Mortification of Sin.* Glasgow: Christian Focus Publications, 2006.

Packer, J.I. *Knowing God.* Downers Grove: Intervarsity Press, 1973.

Peale, Norman Vincent. *The Power of Positive Thinking.* New York: Simon & Schuster, 1952/2003.

Peterson, Eugene (Interview by Mark Galli). "Spirituality for all the Wrong Reasons." *Christianity Today* 49, no.3 (March 2005), 42-47.

Peterson, Eugene H. *Reversed Thunder: The Revelation of John and the Praying Imagination.* New York: HarperOne, 1988.

Plantinga, Cornelius Jr. *Not the Way It's Supposed to Be: A Breviary of Sin.* Grand Rapids: Eerdmans Publishing, 1995.

Pyne, Robert A. *Humanity & Sin.* Nashville: Word Publishing, 1999.

Ryle, JC. *Holiness.* Grange Close, England: Evangelical Press, 1879/2001.

Schreiner, Thomas R. and Ardel B. Caneday. *The Race Set Before Us: A Biblical Theology of Perseverance & Assurance.* Downers Grove: IVP Academic, 2001.

Schuller, Robert H. *Self Esteem: The New Reformation.* Waco: Word Books, 1982.

Slater, Lauren. "The Trouble with Self-Esteem." *The New York Times magazine*. February 3, 2002, accessed online: http://www.nytimes.com/2002/02/03/magazine/the-trouble-with-self-esteem.html; Internet.

Smith, James Bryan. *Rich Mullins: A Devotional Biography: An Arrow Pointing to Heaven*. Nashville: Broadman & Holman Publishers, 2000.

Sproul, RC. *The Holiness of God*. Carol Stream: Tyndale House, 1998.

Stevenson, Mark. "Behold Your God, Recovering the Majesty of God." *Journey Magazine* 7, no. 3 (Winter 2010): 22-29.

Stott, John. *The Contemporary Christian*. Downers Grove: InterVarsity Press, 1992.

Stott, John. *The Cross of Christ*. Downers Grove: InterVarsity Press, 1986.

Stott, John. *The Message of Romans*. Downers Grove: InterVarsity Press, 1994.

Tada, Joni E. and Steve Estes. *When God Weeps*. Grand Rapids: Zondervan, 1997.

Tarrants, Thomas. "Pride and Humility." *Knowing & Doing* (Winter 2011): 3, 14-19.

Tchividjian, Tullian. "The Focus has Shifted," *Liberate website*. January 30, 2015. http://www.pastortullian.com/2015/01/30/the-focus-has-shifted/

Tozer, AW. *Keys to the Deeper Life*. Grand Rapids: Zondervan, 1957/1984.

Tozer, A.W. *The Pursuit of God*. Harrisburg: Christian Publications, 1948.

Tucker, Ruth A. *Walking Away From Faith: Unraveling the Mystery of Belief & Unbelief*. Downers Grove: InterVarsity Press, 2002.

Vincent, Milton. *A Gospel Primer for Christians*. Bemidji, MN: Focus Publishing, 2008.

Voskamp, Ann. *One Thousand Gifts: A Dare to Live Fully Right Where You Are*. Grand Rapids: Zondervan, 2010.

Walvoord John F. and Roy B. Zuck, eds., *The Bible Knowledge Commentary* (New Testament). USA: Victor Books, 1983.

Whitney, Donald S. *Spiritual Disciplines for the Christian Life*. Colorado Springs: Navpress, 1991.

Yancey, Philipp. *Disappointment with God*. Grand Rapids: Zondervan, 1988.

Endnotes

1   *The Power of Positive Thinking* is Peale's most widely read work originally published in 1952.

2   Horowitz provides an extensive history from a secular perspective. Jones & Woodbridge from an evangelical Christian perspective and in connection with the prosperity gospel. Walter Martin's classic book has good content on Swedenborgianism and Christian Science. See bibliography for multiple sources.

3   Mitch Horowitz, *One Simple Idea* (New York: Crown Publishers, 2014), 7.

4   Ibid., 21.

5   Note that this is in conflict with the orthodox Christian teaching of the hypostatic union. Jesus was the God-man. He was *fully* God and *fully* human, two distinct natures in one Person.

6   Prentice Mulford, *Thought are Things* (New York: Barnes & Noble, 1889/2007), 77-86. You can note similarities with the modern-day New Age movement.

7   As quoted in David W. Jones and Russell S. Woodbridge, *Health, Wealth & Happiness* (Grand Rapids: Kregel, 2011), 39.

8   Norman Vincent Peale, *The Power of Positive Thinking* (New York: Simon Schuster, 1952), 86.

9   Ibid., 49 -50.

10 Mitch Horowitz, *One Simple Idea* (New York: Crown Publishers, 2014), 170.

11 Robert Collier as quoted in Rhonda Byrne, *The Secret* (New York: Atria Books, 2006), 165.

12 Philipp Yancey, *Disappointment with God* (Grand Rapids: Zondervan, 1988), 9.

[13] Also see references such as 2 Timothy 3:12; 1 Peter 2:21.

[14] Randy Alcorn, *If God is Good* (Colorado Springs: Multnomah Books, 2009), 381.

[15] "This is my Father's world. O let me ne'er forget that though the wrong seems oft so strong, God is the ruler yet." Hymn from 1901 by Maltbie D. Babcock, "This Is My Father's World"

[16] Paraphrased/summarized from Randy Alcorn, *If God is Good* (Colorado Springs: Multnomah Books, 2009), 14.

[17] Mitch Horowitz, *One Simple Idea* (New York: Crown Publishers, 2014), 189

[18] Evangelical scholars typically interpret Isaiah 14:12-18 and Ezekiel 28:12-19 as referring to more than the earthly kings in question and to the original satanic power behind them.

[19] C.S. Lewis, *Mere Christianity* (Old Tappen: Fleming Revell Company, 1952), 198.

[20] Cornelius Plantinga Jr., *Not the Way It's Supposed to Be* (Grand Rapids: Eerdmans Publishing, 1995), 105.

[21] Isaiah 16:6; Jeremiah 50:29,32; Jeremiah 13:9; Hosea 5:5.

[22] Mark McMinn, *Why Sin Matters* (Wheaton: Tyndale House, 2004), 78.

[23] Ephesians 4:2; James 3:14-16; 1 Peter 5:5; Ephesians 5:21

[24] JD Douglas, ed., *New Bible Dictionary* (Wheaton: Tyndale House, 1982), 966.

[25] Ruth A. Tucker, *Walking Away From Faith* (Downers Grove: InterVarsity Press, 2002), 181.

[26] Jerry Bridges, *The Discipline of Grace* (Colorado Springs: NavPress, 1994), 31.

[27] Maria Konnikova, "Lessons from Sherlock Holmes: Confidence Is Good; Overconfidence, Not So Much" (*Scientific American* blog, September 6, 2011); accessed online: http://blogs.scientificamerican.com/guest-blog/2011/09/06/lessons-from-sherlock-holmes-confidence-is-good-overconfidence-not-so-much/; Internet.

[28] Mark McMinn, *Why Sin Matters* (Wheaton: Tyndale House, 2004), 71.

[29] Adam Alter, "The Powerlessness of Positive Thinking" (*The New Yorker*, February 13, 2014), accessed online: http://www.newyorker.com/business/currency/the-powerlessness-of-positive-thinking; Internet.

30   David W. Jones and Russell S. Woodbridge, *Health, Wealth & Happiness* (Grand Rapids: Kregel, 2011), 40.

31   G.K. Chesterton, *Orthodoxy* (San Francisco: Ignatius Press, 1908), 19.

32   Mark McMinn, *Why Sin Matters* (Wheaton: Tyndale House, 2004), 107.

33   Robert A. Pyne, *Humanity & Sin* (Nashville: Word Publishing, 1999), 171.

34   Joseph Coleson, ed., *Be Holy* (Indianapolis: Wesleyan Publishing, 2008), 15.

35   Cornelius Plantinga Jr., *Not the Way It's Supposed to Be* (Grand Rapids: Eerdmans Publishing, 1995), xiii.

36   A.W. Tozer, *The Pursuit of God* (Harrisburg: Christian Publications, 1948), 45.

37   Robert A. Pyne, *Humanity & Sin* (Nashville: Word Publishing, 1999), 211

38   Brennan Manning, *The Ragamuffin Gospel* (Colorado Springs: Multnomah Books, 1990/2000/2005), 87.

39   As quoted in CJ Mahaney, *Living the Cross Centered Life* (Colorado Springs: Multnomah, 2006), 131.

40   Joni E. Tada and Steve Estes, *When God Weeps* (Grand Rapids: Zondervan, 1997), 60.

41   John F. Walvoord and Roy B. Zuck, eds., *The Bible Knowledge Commentary, New Testament* (USA: Victor Books, 1983), 619.

42   Timothy Dudley-Smith, ed., *Authentic Christianity From the Writings of John Stott* (Downers Grove: Intervarsity, 1995), 168.

43   John Stott, *The Contemporary Christian* (Downers Grove: Intervarsity, 1992), 375.

44   Dietrich Bonhoeffer, *Life Together* (San Fancisco: Harper & Row, 1954), 96.

45   RC Sproul, *The Holiness of God* (Carol Stream: Tyndale House, 1998), 191.

46   Jerry Bridges, *The Discipline of Grace* (Colorado Springs: NavPress, 1994), 40-41.

47   Mitch Horowitz, *One Simple Idea* (New York: Crown Publishers, 2014), 96.

48   Rhonda Byrne, *The Secret* (New York: Atria Books, 2006), 47-54.

49   Gerald R. McDermott, *The Baker Pocket Guide to World Religions* (Grand Rapids: Baker Books, 2008), 25-26.

50   John Stott, *The Contemporary Christian* (Downers Grove: InterVaristy, 1992), 45.

51   Oswald Chambers, *My Utmost for His Highest* (Uhrichsville, Ohio: Barbour, 1935, 1963), Dec. 2 devotional.

52   I have not read it, but this is the title of a Christian book by Eugene Peterson. *A Long Obedience in the Same Direction, Discipleship in an Instant Society* (Downers Grove: InterVarsity Press, 2000).

53   JC Ryle, *Holiness* (Grange Close, England: Evangelical Press, 1879, 2001), 55.

54   As quoted in Ann Voskamp, *One Thousand Gifts* (Eugene: Zondervan, 2010), 171.

55   Randy Alcorn, *If God is Good* (Colorado Springs: Multnomah, 2009), 342.

56   G.K. Chesterton, *Orthodoxy* (San Francisco: Ignatius Press, 1908), 18-19.

57   AW Tozer, *Keys to the Deeper Life* (Grand Rapids: Zondervan, 1957, 1984), 35.

58   Leslie Leyland Fields, "Throwing Christ over the Cliff," *Christianity Today* 56, no. 5 (May 2012): 50.

59   Drew Dyck, "How we Forgot the Holiness of God," *Christianity Today* 58, no. 4 (May 2014): 56.

60   RC Sproul, *The Holiness of God* (Carol Stream: Tyndale House, 1998), 48.

61   JI Packer, *Knowing God* (Downers Grove: Intervarsity Press, 1973), 83.

62   Timothy Keller, *The Freedom of Self-forgetfulness* (Leyland, England: 10Publishing, 2012), 9.

63   Robert H. Schuller, *Self Esteem, The New Reformation* (Waco: Word Books, 1982), 14, 26-27, 36-37. While Schuller attempts to be diplomatic and not neglect core doctrines, the following thoughts from the book speak for themselves: Sin is any act or thought that robs us of our self-esteem (14), "What we need is a theology of salvation that begins and ends with a recognition of every person's hunger for glory" (26-27), theology that begins with God or the Scripture is a problem, rather theology should begin with the dignity of humanity (36-37).

64   Lauren Slater, "The Trouble with Self-Esteem"(*The New York Times* magazine, February 3,2002); available from: http://www.nytimes. com/2002/02/03/magazine/the-trouble-with-self-esteem.html; Internet.

65   Ibid.

66 Humanitarian work worldwide can be viewed as fruit of the Christian view of humanity. For example: life is cheap, and there is little regard for life, in a Hindu religious system that revolves around karma and samsara.

67 Kelly Monroe Kullberg and Lael Arrington, eds., *A Faith and Culture Devotional* (Grand Rapids: Zondervan, 2008), 177.

68 C.S. Lewis, *Mere Christianity* (Old Tappen: Fleming Revell Company, 1952), 204.

69 Thomas Tarrants,"Pride and Humility," *Knowing & Doing* (Winter 2011): 19.

70 Timothy Keller, *The Freedom of Self-forgetfulness* (Leyland, England: 10Publishing, 2012), 32.

71 Ibid., 33.

72 Glenn R. Kreider, *God with Us* (Phillipsburg: P&R Publishing, 2014), 41.

73 James L.R. Catron, *New Testament Survey* (Dubuque: ECS Ministries, 2004), 74.

74 William MacDonald, *Romans the Gospel of Grace* (Dubuque: Emmaus Bible College, 1970), 17.

75 John Stott, *The Message of Romans* (Downers Grove: InterVarsity Press, 1994), 118.

76 The idea expressed succinctly in this sentence is one I came across on the social media platform of a Christian author or pastor, but I am now unable to find the source.

77 Donald S. Whitney, *Spiritual Disciplines for the Christian Life* (Colorado Springs: Navpress, 1991), 230.

78 As quoted in Eugene H. Peterson, *Reversed Thunder* (New York: Harper One, 1991), 42.

79 Stephen Mansfield, *ReChurch* (Brentwood: BarnaBooks, 2010), 59.

80 Dietrich Bonhoeffer, *Life Together* (San Fancisco: Harper & Row, 1954), 110.

81 Statement by Brian McLaren, as quoted in Michael Frost, *Exiles* (Peabody: Hendrickson Publishers, 2006), 104. While I agree with this quote, I am not otherwise endorsing or agreeing with the emergent church perspective.